DANGEROUS CURVES

A BIBLICAL BLUEPRINT FOR MORAL INTEGRITY

Navigating the Hazardous Curves of Your Spiritual Journey

LARRY SCHNEDLER

ISBN 978-1-0980-2685-1 (paperback)
ISBN 978-1-0980-2686-8 (digital)

Copyright © 2020 by Larry Schnedler

All rights reserved. No part of this publication may be reproduced, distributed, or transmitted in any form or by any means, including photocopying, recording, or other electronic or mechanical methods without the prior written permission of the publisher. For permission requests, solicit the publisher via the address below.

Christian Faith Publishing, Inc.
832 Park Avenue
Meadville, PA 16335
www.christianfaithpublishing.com

Unless otherwise indicated, all Biblical texts are taken from the New King James Version (NKJV) of the Bible.

Scripture quotations noted NIV are taken from the Holy Bible: New International Version, copyright © 1973, 1978, 1984 by the Intrnational Bible Society. Used by permission of Zondervan Publishing House. All rights reserved.

All examples cited are true. Names have been changed to protect the identity of the persons involved.

Printed in the United States of America

Praise for Dangerous Curves

I have known Larry and Annis Schnedler for more than fifty years and I am honored that they ask me to write an endorsement for *Dangerous Curves*. I believe this book, when applied to the lives of God's servants, will save many from the shame of moral failure. It's my conviction that it should be read and reread by all who find themselves in any level of ministry. Larry shows us how to live in purity of thought and action, assuring us that the victory Jesus gives over the power of temptation is more than sufficient to keep us from a pit of moral wreckage. I believe this book is one of the most complete ever written on this important subject. **Wayne Myers, president, The Great Commision Evangelistic Association and missionary to Mexico for over seventy years**

Larry Schnedler is the real thing—a genuine apostle who lays his life down for the many churches relating to him. In this book he exposes moral failings of church leaders—a demonic blight that currently threatens the church at large in this and other countries. This much-needed exposé explains why and how these sexual schemes come into being, and how to properly deal with them. This is a must-read for all leaders, those needing restoration, as well as those who want to become effective restorers. **Bruce Gunkle, pastor, City of Refuge Christian Fellowship, San Antonio, Texas**

You are holding in your hands a book that offers hope, healing and answers to those who are truly seeking freedom. Jesus came to set men and women free from every bondage that entangles and traps us—including sexual sin. We are in a spiritual battle. We wrestle not with flesh and blood but with principalities and powers in heavenly places (Ephesians 6:12). I have known and worked with Larry and Annis Schnedler for more than twenty-five years. They have spent their lives teaching leaders, planting churches, and building up God's servants. I believe *Dangerous Curves* was written from a heart of love, not of condemnation or judgment. It is time for the church world-wide to wake up to the schemes of the enemy. This book will help not only those who find themselves trapped in a dark place but also will help us minister more effectively to leaders in trouble. Thank you, Larry, for shining a bright light on this important topic. ***Scott Stanek, pastor, Bastrop Christian Outreach Center, Bastrop, Texas***

I first met Larry and Annis Schnedler in 1965 in Guadalajara, Mexico during my second missionary assignment. Over the years, I have known Larry to be totally committed to the Word of God and its teachings on Moral Purity. That devotion has eminently qualified him to write on this subject. In this book, Larry gives clear answers to the problem of moral failure in leadership. A great general once said, "Leadership is a combination of two powerful elements: strategy and character. If we must dispense with one, it would be strategy." I would add that Jesus is more interested in one's character than his ministry, because without character, one cannot have a true ministry. I recommend that anyone who aspires to serve in the Kingdom of God prayerfully read this book. ***Dr. Stanley A. Black, Missionary Evangelist, Hispanic International Ministries***

I dedicate this book to my wife, Annis, who for fifty-seven years has been an unfailing fountain of encouragement and happiness in my life. As a youth, I was taught, "God gives His best to those who let Him choose." God chose Annis for me—His best. Our marriage has been happy and blessed, "like the days of heaven upon earth" (Deuteronomy 11:21[b]).

I also dedicate this to the Lord Jesus, our best example in life and matchless source of moral purity.

CONTENTS

Acknowledgments 9
Introduction..11

1 Minor Problem or Epidemic?...13
   An alarming number of moral falls and scandals have
   occurred in the body of Christ during the past few years.
   It is no longer a simple problem—it is an epidemic!

2 The Devil's Menu: Varieties of Sexual Sin 21
   Sexual sin takes many forms. Knowing
   them helps to prevent them.

3 Sexual Addiction..36
   When both feet are caught in the trap

4 The Scarlet Sin 41
   What you need to know about adultery

5 The High Cost of Sexual Sin 49
   Those who become ensnared in illicit sex do not realize the
   high price they will pay for the forbidden fruit.

6 Under the Influence: Causes of Moral Failure 67
   We are surrounded by influences that can pull us
   down into a moral quagmire if we are not vigilant.

7 Warning Signs: God's Early Warning System 78
   Just as there are signs on highways warning of danger, God
   has placed warning signs for our sexual and moral life.

8 Myths and Lies We Believe: In Search of Truth 88
   Believing the Spirit of truth or the spirit of error determines
   the quality of our moral life and our destiny.

9   What Every Wife Should Know 97
      The wife is key, and more than anyone else can help
      her husband protect his marriage and his moral life.

10   In Search of Moral Purity 107
      Biblical counsel for living free of sexual sin and
      seeking spiritual, moral and sexual purity.

11   How to Resist Temptation and Finish Well 117
      Boundaries that protect our moral life

ACKNOWLEDGMENTS

First of all, I want to express my gratitude to my wife and life companion, Annis, for her valuable assistance in proofreading and helping with the manuscript and for her ideas and suggestions.

I am also grateful to my sons, Steven and Randy, for their invaluable help in proofreading, suggestions, and encouragement.

INTRODUCTION

When we travel on the streets and highways of our nation, signs warn us of potential danger that may put our life at risk. They alert us to reduce our speed and, in some cases, to stop. The obvious purpose of the signs is to avoid tragedies. The prudent driver pays attention, reduces his speed, and proceeds with caution. One of these signs is *Dangerous Curves*.

As we travel the road of life—especially those of us in leadership—we also find signs that God has placed along the way to save us from moral catastrophes. It's common to see roadside markers—crosses—indicating the place where someone died, probably due to a driver's lack of vigilance. My motive for writing on this kind of topic is to help save servants of God, pastors, leaders, and believers in general from falling into one of the enemy's favorite and most effective traps: the snare of sexual sin.

You may be struggling now with temptation in this area. This book is designed to help you to turn away and avoid a disaster in your life and ministry. The Bible says: "A prudent man foresees evil and hides himself, but the simple pass on and are punished" (Proverbs 22:3). God's will for us is to win over temptation and give a wide berth to "the sin which so easily ensnares us" (Hebrews 12:1[b]).

Or perhaps you think, "Well, that's good for others, but I don't have a problem in that area." It's true that some are more susceptible to this kind of temptation than others, but as we'll see, no one is invulnerable to the possibility of being tempted by sexual sin—no one! An unguarded moment, the right set of circumstances, and unexpected things can and do happen. Many who thought it could never happen to them later found that it *did*.

DANGEROUS CURVES

Pastor and author Bill Perkins says, "If you think you could not be tempted in this area, then you are more saintly that David, stronger than Samson, and wiser that Solomon."[1] And Paul warns "Therefore let him who thinks he stands take heed lest he fall" (1 Corinthians 10:12).

Temptations can be subtle and surprisingly strong. Jesus admonishes us, "Keep alert and pray. Otherwise temptation will overpower you. For the spirit indeed is willing, but how weak the body is!" (Matthew 26:41, TLB)

Others will find valuable assistance—as pastors, counselors, or friends—for helping others that may be navigating some dangerous curves in their lives. Whatever your situation—struggling or helping fellow strugglers—my hope is that you will find in this little book a strengthening hand and an encouraging voice to help avoid the hazardous bends in the road and arrive safely at the destination marked, "Well done, faithful servant." Moral purity and sexual integrity are achievable goals. Don't let the stratagems of the enemy stop you short of that holy ambition. Hopefully you will find in *Dangerous Curves* the help you need to make that a blessed reality in your life.[2]

---

[1] Bill Perkins, *When Good Men Are Tempted* (Zondervan Publishers, 1997, 2007), 88.

[2] Since the majority of those who fall prey to sexual sin are men, most cases shared in the book deal with the masculine sex, and masculine-gender terms are used. However, in the present age, the temptation to infidelity is great, subtle, and growing among women. In fact, there has been a notable increase in this area, especially among young wives (married seven years or less). This is due to an increasing number of women in the workplace and to the Women's Liberation Movement. Therefore, please remember that the same principles that apply to the masculine sex apply also to women.

Likewise, the book speaks often of pastors and other leaders who have experienced moral problems in their lives. The author loves and appreciates pastors and other spiritual leaders and the great work they perform in God's kingdom. Since I have worked with pastors and churches for many years, I have a broader knowledge of the problems and temptations they face. *Dangerous Curves* is in no way an attempt to single them out as more susceptible to temptation than others but rather an effort to help them avoid the traps that have ensnared so many. It is understood, therefore, that principles that apply to pastors and leaders apply equally to all Christians and even nonbelievers.

1

Minor Problem or Epidemic?

For this is the will of God, your sanctification: that you abstain from sexual immorality... For God did not call us to be impure, but to live a holy life.
—1 Thessalonians 4:3, 7 (NKJV)

G. Lloyd Rediger, counselor to pastors, calculates that 10 percent of ministers are guilty of sexual sin and another 15 percent are close to crossing the line.[3]

No one is exempt from the possibility of a moral fall—absolutely no one.

---

[3] G. Lloyd Rediger, quoted in *Ministerial Ethics*, by Joe E. Trull and James E. Carter (Broadman & Holman Publishers), 81.

DANGEROUS CURVES

William was a young pastor, full of enthusiasm for his ministry, and trained as a marriage and family counselor. He was married to a good wife and had three children. His, seemingly, was an exemplary family that was loved and appreciated by his church and community. But William had a problem: he was living in sexual sin. He viewed pornography, frequented massage parlors, and was lustful. He thought his wife did not love him and that he needed and deserved sexual attention from other women. In his counseling, he began to establish emotional and romantic ties with the women who sought his counsel. Such contacts ended in sexual relations with some of the counselees.

Robert was the youth pastor in his church. He fell in love with a young lady from the church, and together they began making wedding plans. Two weeks before his marriage to Martha, he yielded to his lust and had sexual relations with another young woman from the church. His sin was not revealed until after the wedding. As a consequence, he lost his ministry, and his marriage has been very difficult with periods of separation and great turbulence.

Jerry was the pastor of a prosperous church in his city. His affair with a member of the church didn't seem to fully satisfy his "need" of sexual intimacy, and eventually he had another and then another affair going—three at the same time. Each of the women thought she was the only one, and all believed the affair helped their pastor "bringing joy to his life and relieving his stress!"

A pastor friend of mine told me, "I know, by testimony of women who have sought counsel in my church, that in this city, various pastors have committed adultery with those very women."

Newsweek magazine reported that up to 30 percent of pastors have committed adultery.[4] Another study, done by a group of denominational pastors in 1993, revealed that 14 percent of them had committed "sexual conduct inappropriate for a minister," and

---

[4] Kenneth Woodward, "Sex, Morality and the Protestant Minister," *Newsweek*, July 28, 1997, 62.

that 70 percent had counseled at least one woman who had had sexual relations with a pastor.[5]

A study of three hundred pastors conducted by *Leadership Magazine* reported that 33 percent of them admitted to "improper sexual conduct" with someone in their church,[6] 20 percent confessed to having had an emotional or physical affair while in ministry, and 12 percent admitted to having extramarital sexual relations while in ministry.[7]

> *33 percent of pastors admitted to "improper sexual conduct" with someone in their church.*

According to one study, 40 percent of Christian leaders interviewed admitted having problems with pornography. Another study revealed an alarming statistic: 51 percent of pastors said that porn on the Internet was a temptation to them, while 37 percent confessed to an ongoing battle with it. Some 33 percent admitted to having visited a porn website. Eighteen percent said they visited a porn site more than once a week. Focus on the Family has a department for help to pastors and reports that 20 percent of the calls received from pastors have to do with pornography or improper sexual conduct in their own lives.[8]

Before the advent of the Internet, when the main source of pornographic viewing was through hotels' internal television systems, a report revealed that pastors and Christian leaders were the greatest users of the paid service of pornographic television in their rooms. For example, in a convention of the NRB (National Religious Broadcasters), the hotel hosting the event reported that 80 percent of the guests used that service.[9]

---

[5] Kerby Anderson, *Marriage, Family, & Sexuality* (Grand Rapids, Michigan: Kregel Press, 2000), 92. Information taken from the *Journal of Pastoral Care*.
[6] H. B. London, Jr., and Neil B. Wiseman, *Pastors at Greater Risk* (Regal Publishers, 2003), 20.
[7] Ibíd., 238.
[8] Ibíd., 238.
[9] Source unknown.

Twenty-four percent of pastors in the United States have received counseling for their own marriages. Thirteen percent have been divorced. Pastors have the second highest rate of divorce of all the professions.[10] As many as 50 percent affirm they are not satisfied with the sexual intimacy experienced in their marriages.

Evangelist Stephen Olford states that on a certain occasion he was preaching in a conference on faithfulness in ministerial marriages. The Holy Spirit came with great conviction of sin, and hundreds of pastors and leaders came to the front crying. Six of them immediately resigned their pastorates. One was having an affair with his secretary. Another was involved sexually with several women in the church choir. Still another was visiting massage parlors and charging it to the church's credit card.[11]

> *24 percent of pastors in the United States have received counseling for their own marriages.*

For years, a pastor I know had sexual relations with his two sisters-in-law, his wife's sisters. Another pastor, who led a large church in southern United States, had, along with other members of his team, sexual relations with a number of female counselees. Another pastoral leader drugged women who sought counseling with him, putting a substance in their drinks. While they slept, he had sexual relations with them. The pastor of a megachurch, who also exercised leadership in national and international ministries, was trapped in the twin sins of homosexuality and drug abuse. When his activities were discovered, he was dismissed from his church.

---

[10] H.B. London, Jr., and Neil B. Wiseman, *Pastors at Greater Risk* (Regal Publishers, 2003), 86.

[11] Stephen Olford, *The Calling of an Evangelist*, from a message presented by Mr. Olford in Amsterdam in 1986, in the World Congress of Evangelists. The message was entitled: "The Evangelist and the Life of Holiness" (World Wide Publications, 1987), 9.

MINOR PROBLEM OR EPIDEMIC?

Charles, a missionary acquaintance in Central America, divorced his wife to marry a young woman who divorced her husband to marry Charles! Another missionary in a Latin American country boarded city buses full of people to feel sexual pleasure when bumping against female passengers and touching them with his hands.

Tony, the son of a friend of mine, lost his wife when she found a new lover on the Internet. She abandoned her husband and children to pursue her new "love." Henry received a new computer for Christmas. By February, he had spent $100,000 viewing porn on the Internet.

Pastor and author Ted Roberts, who was rescued from a life of sexual addiction and now works with hundreds of men with sexual problems, said that when he visits congregations, he finds that between 50 and 60 percent of the men are struggling to be free of sexual problems.[12]

Christian counselor Russ Willingham affirms that unhealthy sexual habits can become addictive. He estimates that between 40 and 60 percent of church-going men are addicted to Internet pornography, compulsive masturbation, infidelity, or sexual fantasies.[13]

A wife expressed that after her husband became addicted to Internet pornography, he became involved in numerous affairs. Many wives are broken, resentful, and depressed due to failure in the moral life of their husbands. One survey of pastors' wives revealed that 50 percent live depressed by the pressures and problems of pastoral life. When we add to this the torment created by a husband's fall, the result to the wives is devastating.

Of course, there are husbands whose hearts are crushed by the betrayal of their wives. A ministerial colleague of mine, a young pastor, had the bitter experience of being abandoned by his wife, who said she was doing it to "live my own life." In one congregation, twelve husbands were shattered emotionally upon discovering that their wives had had affairs with a leader in the church.

---

[12] H.B. London, Jr., and Neil B. Wiseman, *Pastors at Greater Risk* (Regal Publishers, 2003), 249. Ted Roberts is pastor of the Foursquare Church, Gresham, Oregon.
[13] From a course on *Treating Sexual Addiction*, Light University, Forest, Virginia, 2007, Workbook, 21.

DANGEROUS CURVES

A pastor admitted to acting out sexually, in one form or another, with as many as sixty different persons in his church. Nonetheless, he remained as leader of the congregation for twenty-five years with no one blowing the whistle. A missionary friend of mine in a Latin American country told of finding a married colleague of his in a motel with a strange woman. That man was supposedly in a "spiritual retreat" to "pray and seek God."

Experts tell us that more than 50 percent of marriages that experience infidelity end in divorce, and some say possibly as many as 65 percent. This paints a sad picture of the enormous collateral damage and wreckage our sexual misconduct can cause.[14] The Barna Research Group reports that between 20 and 40 percent of Christian marriages are affected, in some measure, by infidelity.[15]

Peter was pastor of a thriving and growing church. One day while cleaning his yard, he found a discarded porn magazine. After leafing through it for a few moments, he deposited it in the trash. But the images he saw stuck in his mind, and he continued to "see" them mentally, at times during the night. He began to fantasize, imagining what it would be like to experience things he saw in the magazine. His community was replete with prostitution, massage parlors, and X-rated video stores. Little by little he began to visit those sites. Pornography, prostitution, and affairs with other women became part of his lifestyle.

Guilt, fear, and depression pushed Peter to the point of desperation, and he decided to end his life. One night, moments before beginning the service, he sat in his car in front of the church. In a few minutes, he should be inside introducing the guest speaker. But Peter didn't want to be in the church—he wanted to die. A pistol he had acquired was pointed at his temple, and his trembling finger was on the trigger. Tension mounted to a crescendo. Then, by the grace of God, he made a life-changing decision. He placed the gun on the car seat and drove to his house where he poured out his dark and

---

[14] Ibíd., 11.
[15] Barna Research Group, quoted in the course "Healthy Sexuality," Light University, Forest, Virginia.

somber story to his wife. A fierce storm was unleashed for both, but it was also the beginning of restoration of life, marriage, and ministry. Today Peter is restored and in a fruitful ministry, but the cost of straying was enormous—his church, his ministry, his testimony, a marriage at risk, plus the years of recuperation and restoration were all part of the price tag.

Ricardo, a pastor I knew in Latin American, forced his eight-year-old daughter to undress while he touched her body and masturbated. This happened on numerous occasions. When the daughter finally reported it, there was physical violence against her: her father struck her, injuring one of her eyes. The law intervened and a social agency placed the daughter in a special home for a time. Another pastor, from the same country, was accused of fondling young girls, daughters of visitors to his home. In the United States, a Christian leader I know exposed himself before his adolescent stepdaughter. Another leader made his little daughter touch him intimately to produce sexual arousal, an act which occurred many times.

Edward, a well-known prophetic minister in the United States, for years hid a double addiction: alcoholism and homosexuality. Another recognized leader in the body of Christ practiced homosexuality and was even found to be carrying on a homosexual affair with his son-in-law—his daughter's husband! Jonathan, pastor of a prosperous church in a capital city of Latin America, abandoned his wife and children when he fell in love with a young girl in his church. He afterward found himself bereft of a family and without a congregation.

These examples represent only a drop in the ocean of actual cases and demonstrate that we are not simply dealing with a *problem* in the body of Christ but with an *epidemic* that's showing up in all levels of Christian leadership and in all cultures and social strata.

The troubling issue of sexual sin that stalks all—men and women, believers and nonbelievers, people of all ages, cultures, and geographical areas of the planet—appears in many forms and expressions. Temptation is no respecter of persons. In the next chapter, we will see some of the shapes this evil takes. Knowing the enemy and his subtle strategies helps to avoid his traps and find victory in the battle for moral purity.

> *Temptation is no respecter of persons.*

In recent years, the situation has not improved but worsened. In fact, with the Internet, the proliferation of sexually explicit material has increased, making accessibility to it easier than ever. This has only increased temptation and augmented the cases of fallen ministers and believers. Howard Hendricks, Christian educator at Dallas Theological Seminary, carried with him a little notebook with the names of former students and minister friends who had fallen into sexual sin. At one time, he had over a hundred names on that list!

For Reflection

1. Does it surprise you that the problem of sexual sin is so prevalent in the world, especially in churches and Christian circles?
2. Were you aware of the tremendous power and attraction that pornography exerts over people, especially on the Internet?
3. What precautions are you taking to guard your heart and ensure moral purity in your life?
4. Do you agree with the author that sexual sin constitutes an epidemic in the body of Christ? What do you believe is the solution to this problem?
5. What did you feel as you read this chapter: sorrow for fallen believers, censure, condemnation, depression, anger? What do you think would be the appropriate reaction?

2

The Devil's Menu
Varieties of Sexual Sin

Feeling no pain, they let themselves go in sexual obsession, addicted to every sort of perversion.
—Ephesians 4:19 (MSG)

They have stifled their consciences and then surrendered themselves to sensuality, practicing any form of impurity *which lust can suggest.*
—Ephesians 4:19, Phillips

"Any form of impurity" refers to the wide diversity of sexual sins that present temptation. Unfortunately, Christian leaders are not exempt from their "fatal attraction." In this chapter, we'll see some of the forms that sexual sins take, examine their characteristics, and see how to escape their destructive influences.

- *Fornication.* This Biblical but slightly antiquated term is sexual immorality. The Greek is *porneia*, which is derived from *porne* (prostitute).[16] Biblically, it is a general word that includes all kinds of illicit sexual conduct, including: pre-marital sexual relations, homosexuality, prostitution, beastiality, pornography, incest, adultery, lasciviousness, and promiscuity. It is illicit sexual conduct of any kind. Today, "fornication" is commonly used to refer to "recreational sex" among singles, done as a sport or for being unable or unwilling to rein in their passions before marriage. This, of course, reflects the spirit of this age, called the *new morality* and the *sexual revolution.*[17] This view of sexuality rejects as an antique of unenlightened times all moral law concerning sexual conduct and demands total liberty to practice freely and without restraint any type of sexual act. The harvest is thousands of pregnant girls, babies born out of wedlock—many raised without fathers—lives confused and broken with regret and guilt, sexually transmitted diseases, and the proliferation of abortion.

    This also results in youths that beget children but have no clue as to how to be responsible fathers and mothers. A new family, built on the foundation of immorality, has little chance of becoming a stable and lasting home. A young couple, struggling to find harmony in their marriage, told a counselor: "The only thing we have in com-

---

[16] *Strong's Greek/Hebrew Dictionary,* #4202 and 4204.
[17] The "new morality" is nothing new and has been called the "old immorality," because it has existed in human history for aeons. The "sexual revolution" on the other hand represents a shift in attitude regarding the free, unrestrained expression of sexual behavior seen in the last fifty or sixty years. This is manifest in the type of material allowed in TV programs, movies, and other forms of entertainment, in the increase in cohabitation, rejection of traditional marriage, and society's acceptance of gay marriage, etc.

mon is sex." Persons who practice sexual freedom as singles are more apt to be unfaithful in their marriages. In a sense, sexual immorality is unfaithfulness to your future spouse. Many youths, confusing love with lust, fall into this trap. When a teacher asked his class what love is, a young man volunteered: "I feel that love is a feeling one feels when he feels he is going to feel something he has never felt." Marriages built on this kind of shaky understanding seldom endure.

- *Adultery.* Adultery occurs when a married person has sexual relations with a person who is not his or her spouse and is the violation of promises of faithfulness and marital exclusivity. It means disloyalty to the spouse and the betrayal of vows made when uniting in marriage. To have extramarital sexual relations is for a spouse to be disloyal to their promises to protect, care for, and exclusively love the special one they have taken into their life. Adultery and unfaithfulness are terms also used in a spiritual sense in the Bible to refer to the disloyalty of God's people in their relationship to Him. For example, James 4:4 says, "Adulterers and adulteresses! Do you not know that friendship with the world is enmity with God? Whoever therefore wants to be a friend of the world makes himself an enemy of God." God asked the prophet Hosea to marry a woman who would become unfaithful to him so the people could see a prophetic object lesson of their own disloyalty to Him.

Although the majority of cases of adultery occur between married men and single women, it happens in a wide scope of situations. The Bible describes adultery as the betrayal of the covenant of marriage between a man and a woman:

> Yet you say, "For what reason?" Because the Lord has been witness between you and the wife of your youth, with whom you have dealt treach-

erously; Yet she is your companion and your wife by covenant.

> *Adultery…is the violation of vows and promises of faithfulness and exclusivity.*

"Therefore take heed to your spirit, and let none deal treacherously with the wife of his youth" (Malachi 2:14–15). See also Proverbs 2:16–17, where it is the *wife* who is breaking her marriage covenant.

In Jeremiah 29:21–23, adultery was one of the causes of the captivity in Babylon: "because they have done disgraceful things in Israel, have committed adultery with their neighbors' wives" (v. 23). The seventh commandment (Exodus 20:14) declares the prohibition of adultery from day one of Israel's existence as a new nation.

AFFAIRS

Types of *Affairs*

- *The prolonged or ongoing affair.* It may last for weeks, months, or in rare cases, years. Bonds beyond merely emotional ties are formed and include repeated physical intimacy, as though living as husband and wife. Many of these end with hatred, disillusion, blackmail, and emotional and financial bankruptcy.
- *The one-night stand.* This occurs in a moment of temptation and passion, often unpremeditated. It may happen with a person previously unknown, such as meeting a woman in a bar or club. The willingness of both parties soon leads to uncontrolled passion and a sexual encounter. One may be looking for such an opportunity, or be seduced, but the result is the same: a tumble into a pit of moral failure. With some, it may be a one-time event. Others repeat the scene

many times, with different persons. Some call this being addicted to one-night stands. One man who practiced this lifestyle enjoyed a night of pleasure in a hotel with a woman he had just met. When he awoke the following morning, he discovered his "lover" had left. On the bathroom mirror, painted with lipstick were the words, "Welcome to the world of AIDS."

- *The emotional or mental affair.* This type occurs in the mind or feelings of a person, not in the physical (although it often leads to a physical relationship). An illicit relationship is enjoyed with another person in the imagination. Fantasies allow emotional enjoyment of romance or even sexual relations. The "beloved" is held, adored, and enjoyed in the thought life. A mental affair can open the door and prepare the way for physical adultery.

Jesus spoke of this in Matthew 5:28, "But I say to you that whoever looks at a woman to lust for her has already committed adultery with her in his heart." This is why the Bible emphasizes the need to control our thoughts: "Casting down arguments and every high thing that exalts itself against the knowledge of God, bringing every thought into captivity to the obedience of Christ" (2 Corinthians 10:5, NKJV).

Some are not willing to cross the line and go "that far," or perhaps their circumstances impede the practice of physical adultery, but who nonetheless commit it in their hearts. Maybe they think this has no consequences (because it's not physical). Or perhaps they think it's the only way to enjoy a relationship that their heart desires. However, the person who practices it will discover there *are* consequences. A mental or emotional affair (1) is a sign of an unhealthy marriage. Something is awry and lacking in the relationship with one's mate. To fantasize of an illicit relationship with another person does not solve the problem or heal the marriage but only provides a temporary escape from boredom or other problems.

(2) It indicates that something is wrong in our heart. The desire for something God prohibits is evidence that a spirit of rebellion is

working in us. We come to believe that the state in which we find ourselves (marriage in general or our particular marriage) is not what we really want, and we search for that "something more." This was the deception the serpent sold to Eve in Eden: "God didn't give you what you deserve; he has deceived you; what you have is not what you could and should have." To us, he adds: "The wife (or husband) you have is not what you need; you deserve more."

> *A mental affair can open the door and prepare the way for physical adultery.*

We can buy into the lie, thinking the mate we have is not adequate or "right." We feel cheated and search for that "something more" that we really "deserve." And like Eve, we take the bait. The real deception is in the lie we believe, not in what God has given us.

Emotional or mental adultery is simply the search for something not given to us by God (someone other than our mate), but something we lust for. The Ten Commandments prohibit, firstly, the act of adultery (seventh commandment), and secondly, even the desire for the wife of another man: "You shall not covet…your neighbor's wife" (tenth commandment, see Exodus 20:14, 17). The desire for something other than what we have been given is a manifestation of man's rebellion against God: the desire to live independent of Him and to decide and follow our own way.

(3) Emotional and mental adultery can easily occur in opposite-sex friendships. When reaching a certain level, the closeness of friendship can create an emotional connection that allows the sharing of personal and marital problems. This can create a growing affection, which, as we saw earlier, is just a step away from physical intimacy.

A mental affair can open the door and prepare the way for a physical one. The law of diminishing returns applies: When certain drugs no longer satisfy, stronger ones are needed to match the former "high" and bring new satisfaction and pleasure. Something similar happens in an emotional relationship that has ceased to be a simple "friendship." Conversations and feelings become "innocent" physical touches. Then come loving caresses, and finally, intimate touches that end in a full-blown sexual relationship. Like dope, sexual sin requires increasingly stronger doses and always takes us farther than we had planned to go.

> *Sexual sin requires stronger and stronger "doses" and always takes us farther than we had planned to go.*

Moral purity begins in the heart. Not only must the physical area remain pure and "the bed undefiled" (Hebrews 13:4) but also the arena of the mind as sacred and inviolable ground. Adultery, whether physical or mental, is a thief that robs the marriage of the happiness it is designed to produce. The Bible warns in Proverbs 4:23: "Keep your heart with all diligence, for out of it spring the issues of life." Wise is the one who guards his or her heart from this and all expressions of sexual impropriety and takes every renegade thought captive in obedience to Christ.

Perversions

Something "perverted" is, according to the dictionary, changed, corrupted, or vitiated, which means to impair the value or quality of something. It is that which has exchanged its original form and purpose for new forms and purposes. In the Old Testament, the Hebrew word for *iniquity* is sometimes translated as "twisted" or "perverted." An example is Jeremiah 3:21 that says, "A voice was heard on the desolate heights, weeping and supplications of the children of Israel. For they have perverted their way; They have forgotten the Lord their God" (NKJV). The NLT says, "They have forgotten the Lord their God and wandered far from his ways." To pervert, then, is to twist, make crooked, corrupt, or change something from its original, to another (less valuable), form or purpose.

The apostle Paul rebuked Elymas, a sorcerer, who was hindering Paul's presentation of the gospel, saying to him, "O full of all deceit and all fraud, you son of the devil, you enemy of all righteousness, will you not cease *perverting* the straight ways of the Lord" (Acts 13:10, author's emphasis)? Jesus was falsely accused of *"perverting* the nation," of telling people not to pay taxes to the Roman government (Luke 23:2). And in Luke 23:14, he is accused of *misleading* the people (same Greek root as above). In Acts 20:30, Paul speaks of depraved leaders in the Ephesus church who would "speak *perverse* things, to draw away the disciples after themselves" (author's emphasis). In Galatians 1:6–7, he warns of false teachers who "want to *pervert* the gospel of Christ" (author's emphasis). Finally, in Philippians 2:15 he exhorts God's people to "shine as lights in the world…in the midst of a crooked and *perverse* generation" (author's emphasis).

The Greek words translated "perverse" in these verses mean "to transform into something of an opposite character, to turn inside out, to change entirely, to turn aside, to corrupt" (*Vine's Expository Dictionary of New Testament Words*).

Romans 1 reveals the tendency of man to pervert or exchange God's divine order for his own, and to substitute God's original design with another. Romans 1:23 says they *"changed* the glory of the incorruptible God into an image made like corruptible man—and birds and four-footed beasts and creeping things." Idolatry is the perversion of the worship of the true God. Verse 25 explains how men *"changed* the truth of God for the lie." Many beliefs embraced by unregerate man are the perversion of God's eternal, unchanging truth (author's emphasis).

- *Homosexuality.* A sexual relationship between two men or two women (lesbianism). Although to many, it may seem normal and justified, God's opinion is different. He calls it an "abomination" (Leviticus 18:22, 20:13; Judges

19:22–23). In Romans 1:24–29, it is called "uncleanness," "vile passions," "lust," "shameful," "against nature," "error," "unrighteousness," and "sexual immorality."

> *The Bible is clear, defining it as something outside God's plan for human sexuality.*

Modern societies increasingly view homosexuality with acceptance and approval, including the legalization of same-sex marriage. Some religious denominations approve these marriages. A number of pastors and bishops have openly declared their homosexuality and have been allowed to continue in their office. Though it is difficult to understand how a pastor or Christian leader could participate in a relationship prohibited by God, sadly it does happen. Many justify it, believing it to be a "natural tendency," that a person is born with that sexual orientation, and there is little or nothing that can change it. But the Bible is clear, defining it as something outside of God's plan for human sexuality.

An educated man in India, upon hearing an exposition of Romans 1, commented, "The man who wrote that surely knows India." The same could be said of many other nations. Someone has called homosexuality "one of the marks of a decadent civilization." At the height of their power, the Persian, Roman, and Greek empires approved of the practice, which some historians believe contributed to their moral collapse. And some historians affirm that fourteen of the first fifteen Roman emperors were homosexuals, including Nero.

The apostle Paul told the Corinthians,

> Do you not know that the unrighteous will not inherit the kingdom of God? Do not be deceived. Neither fornicators, nor idolaters, nor adulterers, nor homosexuals (catamites, those submitting to homosexuals), nor sodomites (male homosexuals)...will inherit the kingdom of God. (1 Corinthians 6:9–10)

Then Paul continues in verse 11, "And such were some of you. But you were washed, but you were sanctified, but you were justified in the name of the Lord Jesus and by the Spirit of our God." For the person who desires, it is possible to be free from homosexuality. This is in no way a condemnation of gay persons; it is simply sharing what the Bible teaches about the practice. God loves homosexuals (and so should we), but He does not love or approve of the practice. In this, the Bible is clear. Acceptance or rejection of it depends upon one's acceptance or rejection of the Bible as God's Word and our final authority.

- *Transgenderism.* This "perversion" (change from original design) allows a male to say: "I'm a woman trapped in a man's body," or a woman to say, "I'm a man trapped in a woman's body." Through special surgeries people can change their sex from masculine to feminine or vice versa. Others simply opt to mentally become a person of the other sex, adopting a new identity by changing their dress, lifestyle, and name. This is another way of changing God's original design, which says, "He that made them at the beginning, made them male and female" (Matthew 19:4).

Other Forms of Illicit Sex

- *Pornography* The root of this word is *porneia*, a Greek work mentioned above, and related to "fornication." In today's world, a plethora of pornographic material is readily available. Even children can be easily exposed to it. In the United States, it is an eight-billion-dollar-a-year business.

> *It's well known that there are between thirty and sixty thousand pornographic websites.*

THE DEVIL'S MENU

Internet. Besides magazines, videos, etc., another means of viewing porn is the Internet, which has been called "cybersex" and "the crack cocaine of sexual addictions." It's well known that there are between thirty thousand and sixty thousand pornographic websites on the net, and it is reported that twenty million American adults log onto those websites regularly.[18] The average age for a child's first exposure to Internet porn is eleven, and 90 percent of youths ages eight to sixteen have viewed online porn, often while doing homework. In a Christian men's conference, a survey found that 53 percent of the men had viewed pornography during the prior week. A sad note is that the number of Christian men that view pornography actually mirrors the national average.

What's Wrong with Porn?

- ➢ Often porn is a gateway or a step into other types of sexual sin. It feeds your sexual energy and often leads to acting out sensual desires.
- ➢ It presents women as sexual objects to be exploited and used but not loved.
- ➢ It exposes good men to that which is unnatural and artificial.
- ➢ It creates a sexuality that is unreal, idealized, and impossible to equal in real life. (A wife may be rejected because she doesn't measure up to what the husband is seeing and desiring.)
- ➢ It gives the impression that sex is something to be enjoyed apart from true love and commitment.
- ➢ It teaches that sex with anyone is okay and normal.

- • *Lust.* This is not so much a practice as a condition lurking in the heart, but it is wrong, nonetheless. It is the womb in which moral sins are conceived and the platform upon

---

[18] Barna Research Group, cited in the course "Healthy Sexuality," Light University, Forest, Virginia.

which they are performed. In 1 John 2:16, it is called "the lust of the flesh" and "the lust of the eyes."

> *Lust is the vile energy that drives men to these acts.*

Lust is an intense and inappropriate longing for something or someone. According to pastor Charles Stanley, lust is desire out of control. It is coveting something which it is not God's will for us to have. A heart full of lust can prepare the life for a moral fall. Sex becomes an obsession rather than a healthy expression of sexuality. Lust leads to the acting out of moral evils such as pornography, abuse of minors, moral impurity, lasciviousness, incest, premarital sex, and adultery. Lust is the vile energy that drives men to these acts.

- *Exhibitionism.* This aberration involves the exposing of the naked body, or sexual parts thereof, in public or before other persons in inappropriate circumstances. It is often practiced with children, perhaps because the exhibitionist believes they are defenseless and will not cause problems. It is an example of what the Bible calls lasciviousness, or impurity. It is indecent exposure, committed by persons incapable or unwilling to exercise their sexuality in an appropriate way.
- *Fantasies.* Undressing a person in our minds, we try to imagine "what it would be like" to have him or her as spouse (or "lover") and to experience an intimate relationship with them. To fantasize is to live an imaginary life with a person who is not our spouse, as though they were. It is unleashing the mind to enjoy sexual intimacy with a person who is "out of reach" in real life.

THE DEVIL'S MENU

> *To fantasize is to live an imaginary life with a person who is not our spouse.*

How do fantasies originate? When a person is not capable of maintaining a normal, healthy relationship with others, for whatever reason, the mind creates situations and scenes in which the person can experience the joy of an imaginary relationship. A fantasy, then, is the creation in the mind of pleasant, sensual experiences that a person does not, should not, or cannot have in real life.

- *Sexual Abuse.* Many are the cases, reported and unreported, of fathers, stepfathers, uncles, older brothers, babysitters, etc., who engage in this evil. This abuse consists of (1) touching and fondling, (2) making inappropriate comments, (3) exhibitionism, and (4) in extreme cases, rape. It occurs primarily with small or adolescent girls, and often, as in the case of homosexual acts, with boys. Victims often suffer from low self-esteem and receive wounds that affect them in future life. Boys are sometimes lured or pushed into a life of homosexuality, and abused girls may later find it difficult to trust men or to relate to their husbands in normal and healthy sexual intimacy. Abused people often become abusers later in life.
- *Sexual Harassment.* It often occurs in the workplace. It may come from a boss or other person of authority who uses his position to seek sexual favors in exchange for a raise in salary, better working conditions, or simply to maintain the employment. A woman can risk her job or fall into disfavor with her boss if she does not cooperate. In the movie *Forrest Gump*, Forrest's mother gave these "favors" to a schoolteacher in exchange for a passing grade for her son. Sexual harassment can occur in any context, including the church, the school, or the home.
- *Wife Swapping.* In this game, several couples meet for an evening of fun and socializing. At the end, the men put

their key rings in a hat, and the wives draw a ring from the hat. Each then goes to spend the night with the owner of the key ring she draws. It is an embellished form of adultery.

- *Prostitution.* This "oldest profession in the world" is the use of one's body in sexual practices to generate financial or other gain or favors. It can take several forms: (1) one may choose such a life, (2) human trafficking, or imposed prostitution, forces girls into it in some parts of the world, or (3) a woman may work in prostitution as the only way she feels she can provide for herself and her children. In any case, it is a practice that lures millions of men into illicit sex. Proverbs 23:27 says, "For a harlot is a deep pit, and a seductress is a narrow well." And Proverbs 22:14a says, "The mouth of an immoral woman is a deep pit." Of course, women aren't the only prostitutes; males also practice it in some scenarios. It was common in Old Testament pagan temple worship.

> *Sin is the attempt to satisfy legitimate needs in illegitimate ways.*

- *Masturbation.* Some persons (women as well as men) are slaves to this practice; sometimes masturbating several times a day. Some practice it using porn, fantasies of persons they would like to have sexual relations with, lustful thoughts, etc. Dr. Mark Laaser in his book *Healing the Wounds of Sexual Addiction*[19] tells of a young man, a patient at his clinic, who masturbated many times every day. He also relates the case of a woman who viewed sexual images on the Internet while masturbating. She did this for years and damaged her body to the point of needing surgery to repair the damage.[20]

---

[19] Dr. Mark Laaser, *Healing the Wounds of Sexual Addiction* (Zondervan, 1992, 1996, 2004), 34.
[20] Dr. Mark Laaser. Comments from the course *Treating Sexual Addiction*, Light University, Forest Virginia, Study Manual, 44.

This practice contributes nothing to the sexual health of a person, or to a healthy marriage. It can be an unhealthy practice, especially when:

- ✓ it's a compulsive habit, or an obsession;
- ✓ it takes the place of and substitutes for a normal intimate relationship with one's spouse;
- ✓ it consumes time and energy needed for healthy and profitable activities;
- ✓ it's accompanied by pornography;
- ✓ it's practiced with mental fantasies of having sex with a person who is not our spouse;
- ✓ it goes against our conscience, producing guilt and other negative emotions.

This is not an exhaustive list of sexual sins but is sufficient for giving a clear idea of what unhealthy sexuality is. Those who seek a life of moral purity will be on guard and avoid them. They will commit their sexuality—a gift from God—to conformity with His plan as elucidated in His Word, the Bible. God has a moral law. Happy are those who follow it.

For Reflection

1. Do you battle with a sin mentioned in this chapter? Which one?
2. Is your battle centered in the mental arena (fantasies, lustful thoughts, wrong desires, etc.) or in the physical area (masturbation, premarital sex, affairs, exhibitionism, etc.)?
3. If you battle with a sexual sin, do you also struggle with guilt, depression, or fear? Do you long to be free from these destructive emotions?
4. Were you ever abused sexually, physically, or emotionally in your childhood or youth? If so, how do you think this may have affected you in relation to your sexuality?

3

Sexual Addiction
When Both Feet Are Caught in the Trap

Most assuredly, I say to you, whoever commits sin is a slave of sin.
—John 8:34

When considering the problem of addiction, there exist three levels:

1. those who commit sexual sins but are not sex addicts;
2. Sex addicts; and

3. sexual offenders: rapists, those having sexual relations or committing sexual abuse with minors, etc. It involves illegal or criminal activity.

Note: It's important to recognize that (1) one can commit sexual sins without being an "addict" and (2) one can be a sexual addict without being an offender and committing criminal acts.

Sexual addiction occurs when one loses control over a sexual behavior. Often the person feels guilt or shame and determines not to repeat the act. However, he feels helpless to stop and soon finds himself continuing to commit the act over and over. No matter how much he wants to discontinue, he is defeated by the lure and attraction of the practice. What are the signs that alert us when addiction is occurring?

> *Sexual addiction occurs when one loses control over a sexual behavior.*

Signs of Sexual Addiction

1. Addicts don't possess the necessary strength to control their compulsive behavior. They feel controlled by a power that is superior to them and that they can no longer manage. Compulsion is "an irresistible impulse to act, regardless of the rationality of the motivation" (*American Heritage Dictionary*).
2. Addicts feel shame for their secret activities and attempt to keep them hidden. They begin to live a double life: sexual enslavement on one hand and a normal, healthy public life on the other.
3. Though they may feel shame or guilt afterward, they experience euphoria and arousal during each sexual activity.

4. Many sex addicts experienced emotional, physical, or sexual abuse in their childhood. Eighty-one percent were abused sexually, 75 percent, physically, and 97 percent suffered emotional abuse in childhood.[21]
5. Addicts experience highs and lows in their emotions, fluctuating between euphoria and depression.
6. Due to their compulsive behavior, addicts often violate the ethical norms of their profession, whether physicians, lawyers, ministers, or public servants, such as political figures. This makes sexual addiction a major issue on two levels: it is a social as well as a personal problem.
7. Often addicts' activities are carried out in isolation, without significant relationships with others. They may find it difficult to maintain healthy relationships due to shame, feelings of unworthiness, or fear of discovery.
8. Sex addicts continue their aberrant activities in spite of the great harm they may be doing: loss of employment, a struggling marriage, jail time, financial ruin, or other damage. They may lose their ability to exercise sound judgment and make wise decisions, though it may lead to economic disaster. A pastor racked up $40,000 on his credit card from porn and prostitution charges due to his addiction. When he couldn't pay the debt, he purchased a gun and began to rob banks. (He had worked in a bank and knew how to pull off a robbery "more successfully.") After a few heists, he was arrested and spent eight years in a federal prison. Another man spent $75,000 viewing porn on the Internet, in one month! Still another spent some $3 million on prostitution during his lifetime. Of course, all cases aren't this extreme, but it offers us an idea of the incredible magnetic, binding, and blinding power a sexual addiction can have in a life.

---

[21] Dr. Mark Laaser. Comments in a video course on *Treating Sexual Addiction*, Light University, Forest Virginia, Student Manual, 44.

SEXUAL ADDICTION

9. The sexual activity becomes an obsession for the person, who spends much time thinking, planning, and fantasizing about the next episode.
10. For many addicts, the sexual activities act as a drug to escape wounds and feelings of pain and loneliness. The effect is similar to that produced by alcohol and narcotics.

Any form of sexual sin can become addictive: masturbation, pornography, affairs, fantasies, fornication, or exhibitionism. Sexual addiction is a substitute for genuine and legitimate intimate relationships. It is estimated that 50 percent of sex addicts are also alcoholics. Most have another kind of addiction as well. When a person exhibits compulsive behavior that persists, notwithstanding repeated attempts to stop, and in spite of harmful and damaging consequences, it's clearly an addiction. There are two kinds of addictions: (1) substance (alcohol, drugs, etc.) and (2) behavior. I don't believe we can claim victimhood for either kind of addiction. We are responsible for our conduct.

Regardless of our past experiences, there is help in God. Christ is the great *Liberator!* He awaits the opportunity to break the chains of any obsession or addiction. Without God in his or her life, the addict has reason to despair. But with Christ, we have access to the greatest power in the universe. We who are called to be light must walk and live in the light.

> God is light and in Him there is no darkness at all. If we say that we have fellowship with Him, and walk in darkness, we lie and do not practice the truth. But if we walk in the light as He is in the light, we have fellowship with one another, and the blood of Jesus Christ His Son cleanses us from all sin. (1 John 1:5–7)

Experts in the field of addictions tell us that self-deception and denial are our greatest enemies. Since sexual addictions are often carried out in secret, coming to the light of God's truth is liberating. Instead of hiding in the darkness, one can bring his or her needs to Christ, the light of the world. He dispels the darkness by shining the light of His Word into the shadowy corners of the heart, revealing unwanted tenants and giving the power to evict them.

We have been considering various types of sexual sins and addictions that can devastate the life of a man or woman not vigilant of their moral state. In the next chapter, we will focus in more depth on the trap that has ensnared many good people, even pastors and spiritual leaders: marital infidelity, the "scarlet sin."

For Reflection

1. How would you define sexual addiction?
2. Why do sexual addicts persist in their destructive behavior when consequences are causing pain in their lives and the lives of others?
3. What are some of the signs that a person is addicted to a sexual practice?
4. Should sex addicts see themselves as "victims?" Why or why not?
5. What do you think of the assertion, "Sexual addiction is a substitute for a genuine, legitimate, and intimate relationship"?
6. In what way is sexual addiction like a drug?

4

The Scarlet Sin
What You Should Know about Adultery

*Whoever commits adultery with a woman lacks
understanding; He who does so destroys his own soul.*
—Proverbs 6:32

*I believe there are as many cases of infidelity
in society as traffic accidents.*[22]
—Dr. Frank Pittman,
psychiatrist and family counselor

---

[22] Dr. Frank Pittman, *Private Lies, Infidelity and the Betrayal of Intimacy* (New York, Norton, 1989), 117. Quoted in *Marriage, Family, & Sexuality* by Kerby Anderson (Grand Rapids, Michigan: Kregel Press, 2000), 92.

DANGEROUS CURVES

During the colonial days of the United States, there was a rule of moral conduct that obligated a woman who had committed adultery to wear, while in public, a scarlet-colored dress. Hence the phrase: *the scarlet sin*. We can imagine the shame she felt, being seen by neighbors and fellow citizens as she moved about in public. And we can imagine her joy when she was released to discard the scarlet dress, forgiven and restored. She was pardoned but probably would not soon forget the high price she paid for her folly.

Why is adultery so censured in the Bible? Why does God hate infidelity so passionately? (It's the one sexual sin mentioned in the Ten Commandments.) How does it trap so many victims, including Christian leaders, who "as an ox being led to the slaughter," blindly follow the enticement of pleasure, only to receive the bitterness of gall as a reward? Why do the attraction and seduction of infidelity seem so irresistible to the tempted person? Why is marital unfaithfulness so accepted and "normal" in modern societies? In this chapter, we'll explore and try to answer these questions, making use of the Bible's counsel and the experiences of fallen leaders.

Why Is Infidelity So Wrong?

- Adultery is a foolish and senseless act with grave consequences. The NIV Spanish version of Proverbs 6:32 says, "He who commits adultery lacks brains; he who acts thus destroys himself." It is common to hear expressions such as these from fallen leaders: "Oh, the foolish and senseless things I have done" and, "How could I have committed such absurd and stupid acts?" But as someone has said, "Only a fool desires what he cannot have."
- Adultery and fornication are no respecters of persons; they affect every stratum of society: rich and poor, good and bad, Christians and nonbelievers. And all the world's societies practice them. Dr. Helen Fisher, an anthropologist, made a study of forty-two diverse societies from all parts

- of the world. Her conclusion? "Adultery occurs in every one, whether pagan or Christian. Marital unfaithfulness was present in all, even the ones where it is punished by death."[23]
- Adultery is believed by some experts to be the number one cause of divorce. Dr. Frank Pittman has written that marital unfaithfulness wrecks marriages and damages children. After thirty years of counseling couples with marital problems, he says he has only seen a handful of divorces where adultery was not involved. Pittman also affirms that the probability of a first marriage ending in divorce is minimal, unless unfaithfulness is involved.[24]

> *Adultery is believed by some experts to be the number one cause of divorce.*

Facts About Unfaithfulness

- At first, sexual sin is attractive but is like fruit that is sweet in the mouth and bitter in the stomach. The pitiful and disastrous picture of Samson at the end of his life, with blindness, slavery, and shame is very different from the earlier picture of euphoria in his sensuality and liaisons with Delilah and other promiscuous women.

   Proverbs 7:4–5 says it with eloquence: "Say to wisdom, 'You are my sister,' and call understanding your nearest kin, that they may keep you from the immoral woman,

---

[23] Helen Fisher, PhD. Taken from her book: *Anatomy of Love* and quoted in *Sex, a Man's Guide*, by Stefan Bechtel and Laurence Roy Stains (Emmaus, Pennsylvania: Rodale Press, Inc.), 427.

[24] Dr. Frank Pittman. Data taken from his book *Private Lies* and quoted in *Sex, a Man's Guide*, por Stefan Bechtel and Laurence Roy Stains (Emmaus, Pennsylvania: Rodale Press, Inc.), 429. Dr. Pittman is a psychiatrist in Atlanta, Georgia.

from the seductress who flatters with her words." Proverbs 5:1–3 describes the temptation, the "honey," of promised pleasures and seductive words: "My son, pay attention to my wisdom; Lend your ear to my understanding, that you may preserve discretion, and your lips may keep knowledge. For the lips of an immoral woman drip honey, and her mouth is smoother than oil."

But verse 4 sounds an alarm against taking the bait: "But in the end she is bitter as wormwood, sharp as a two-edged sword." The NIV says, "But in the end she is bitter as gall, sharp as a double-edged sword." Ecclesiastes 7:26 echoes the warning: "I find more bitter than death the woman who is a snare, whose heart is a trap and whose hands are chains. The man who pleases God will escape her, but the sinner she will ensnare" (NIV).

Persons who take the bait of sexual sin are living in an imaginary world of fantasies, lies, and a bubble of deceit. When the bubble bursts and that world comes crashing down, dreams become nightmares, and the mirage, an arid desert.

- If a leader who is living in sin experiences growth and prosperity in his or her ministry, it should not be taken as a sign of God's approval of their conduct. A pastor whom I knew and who was regularly committing adultery expressed: "The blessing of God is evident in my ministry, and that is evidence that God is not against what I am doing."

What an erroneous conclusion! A pastor in Texas experienced growth and blessing in his church, needing three Sunday services to accommodate the crowds. However, his lifestyle was far from having God's approval, as he learned when his homosexuality was discovered and he was dismissed from his pastorate. If God blesses a ministry in this type of situation, it is by His mercy and love for the people, not because He approves of the conduct of the leader.

THE SCARLET SIN

> *Temptation would have fewer "takers"*
> *if the consequences were immediate.*

- Sexual sin gives birth to other sins. Lying, deceiving, manipulation, hypocrisy, coverup, a double life, self-deception, and other vices always accompany immorality. In the case of King David, it even included murder!
- Adultery—and all sexual sin—will be judged by God. Of course, judgment seldom falls immediately. Charles Spurgeon said that temptation would have fewer "takers" if the consequences were immediate. But delay does not mean cancellation. Hebrews 13:4 declares, "Marriage should be honored by all, and the marriage bed kept pure, for God will judge the adulterer and all the sexually immoral." (NIV).

First Thessalonians 4:6 says, "that no one should take advantage of and defraud his brother in this matter [adultery with another man's wife], because the Lord is the avenger of all such, as we also forewarned you and testified" (author's note). The NIV says, "The Lord will punish men for all such sins." Verse 7 states, "For God did not call us to be impure, but to live a holy life" (NIV).

The prophet Malachi pronounced judgment on those who practiced adultery, "And I will come near you for judgment; I will be a swift witness against sorcerers, against adulterers" (3:5). And Paul reminds us, "For we must all appear before the judgment seat of Christ, that each one may receive the things *done* in the body, according to what he has done, whether good or bad" (2 Corinthians 5:10).

Of course, when there is true repentance, God forgives our sin (see 1 John 1:7, 9). The ideal—and what God expects of us—is that we judge ourselves (judge our conduct as inappropriate and unacceptable), followed by repentance and separation from all contact with persons or situations related to the illicit relationship. The woman Jesus called "Jezebel" in the Thyatira church was guilty of fornication and adultery and of seducing God's servants. In Revelation 2:21,

Jesus says, "And I gave her time to repent of her sexual immorality, and she did not repent."

> *When there's true repentance,*
> *God forgives our sin.*

When a person is caught in the web of an illicit relationship, God, in His mercy, allows time to repent, placing warning signs before them. He calls and waits for them to change, as in the case of the wicked woman, Jezebel. But when the person doesn't heed the signs and persists unrepentant in their sin, God, at some point, intervenes.

God's Three Options

First Corinthians 11:31–32 gives us an important principle: "For if we would judge ourselves, we would not be judged. But when we are judged, we are chastened [disciplined] by the Lord, that we may not be condemned with the world" (author's note). These are God's three options:

1. *We judge ourselves.* If we do this and truly repent, God will not have to judge and discipline us: "If we would judge ourselves, we would not be judged" (v. 31). In this case, we will have judged and corrected our actions, sparing ourselves the pain of divine intervention.
2. *We are judged and disciplined by God.* If we persist in our sin, with no intentional self-discipline and repentance, God has to intervene. He takes over the judging and disciplining. This normally occurs when our sin is discovered by others and revealed. At this point, we face a crucial decision: repent and accept God's discipline or rebel and stubbornly refuse His loving correction and restoration. The person

THE SCARLET SIN

who refuses to repent under God's hand of love will feel His hand in discipline and judgment of sin.

3. *Be condemned with the world.* When a man hardens his heart, refuses to repent, and continues in his sin, he is on a slippery slope. God's discipline is for restoring, not condemning, us. It is "that we may not be condemned with the world" (v. 32).

> *God's patience does have its limits.*

If we practice step 1, steps 2 and 3 are unnecessary. If not, we will experience God's intervention. He is loving and patient. However, His patience *does* have limits.

A Christian leader who had fallen into a life of immorality visited a church. There, a person who knew neither him nor his situation spoke a prophetic word, which said, in essence, "There is a person present in this meeting to whom I have called and waited. This is the last opportunity you have to repent." The man, however, turned a deaf ear to the message and left the meeting. Shortly afterward, he was involved in an accident that took his life. We should not interpret the time God gives us to repent, as permission to continue in our sin!

If we judge ourselves in time, that is, recognize that what we are doing is sin and extremely displeasing and unacceptable to God, we can save ourselves the pain and disgrace of a moral fall, including the shame of being judged and disciplined by God. "He who covers his sins will not prosper, but whoever confesses and forsakes them will have mercy" (Proverbs 28:13). The "scarlet sin" and other sexual misdeeds will not trap and enslave us if we follow God's directives. The choice is whether to let Him wash away the "scarlet" with the blood of Christ and make it "white as snow" or let it remain "red like crimson" (see Isaiah 1:18).

What is the cost of a moral fall? Why is a person, especially a leader, willing to risk and sacrifice so much—reputation, ministry, testimony, character, family—for so little that is transitory and superficial? In the next chapter, we'll explore the answers to these questions and the high price of sexual sin.

For Reflection

1. Do you believe Samson considered the cost of a moral fall? In your opinion, how should Samson have conducted himself as he faced these sexual temptations?
2. Can a Christian leader take success and the "apparent blessing of God" as approval of wrong conduct?
3. Which of the three options of 1 Corinthians 11:31–32 do you believe is preferable? Why?
4. What happens to persons who are living in sin and refuse to judge themselves and even refuse God's discipline?

5

The High Cost of Sexual Sin
Sin Now, Pay Later—but Payment *Will* Come Due

Be sure your sin will find you out.
—Numbers 32:23 (NKJV)

*When wickedness comes, so does contempt,
and with shame comes disgrace.*
—Proverbs 18:3 (NIV)

Consideration of the plethora of sex scandals, plus the staggering costliness of illicit sex should be an adequate deterrent for halting any improper behavior in our life. But we seem to believe we can sin "on credit," without paying now and "To heck with the future.

I can handle that when the time comes." Or perhaps we don't think about the future at all. The important thing now is the pleasure we need, the irresistible lure of the temptation. But sooner or later, the bill will arrive, demanding payment. The bill is high and charges interest to boot (collateral damage). Not only is our life or ministry or character or marriage marred, but others are affected by our misdeeds. Sin will demand its price, and the cost is very high, as we'll see in this chapter.

How certain is it that we will not escape the consequences of our sin? How sure is it that the sun will rise tomorrow morning? The Bible speaks of the "deceitfulness of sin," making us believe that "no one will know, and there will be no consequences for the act, at least nothing we can't handle."

> *Sin will demand its price, and*
> *the cost is very high.*

But the Bible is clear:

> Do not be deceived, God is not mocked; for whatever a man sows, that he will also reap. For he who sows to his flesh will of the flesh reap corruption, but he who sows to the Spirit will of the Spirit reap everlasting life. (Galatians 6:7–8)

All human arguments stacked against the Word of God crumble and fall, like the walls of Jericho. God's eternal, unchanging Word is our final authority.

What Is the Cost of Sexual Sin?

In the Old Testament, the price of adultery was steep: death.

THE HIGH COST OF SEXUAL SIN

> If a man is found lying with a woman married to a husband, then both of them shall die—the man that lay with the woman, and the woman; so you shall put away the evil from Israel. (Deuteronomy 22:22).

In ancient times, the punishment for adultery was severe, even in other cultures and societies.

- ➢ The Hammurabi Code (Mesopotamia, 1800 BC) demanded the death penalty for offenders, by being drowned in a river.
- ➢ In Greek and Roman societies, an adulteress could be punished with death, but for men, there was no such severe punishment.
- ➢ As mentioned earlier, during colonial days in the United States, a woman guilty of adultery was made to wear a scarlet-colored dress in public to announce to all the shamefulness and opprobrium of her sin. A prostitute was called a "scarlet woman." And a husband could kill with impunity the man who committed adultery with his wife. One of Elvis Presley's songs contained this line (paraphrased): *Play around some and you could lose your wife. Play around some more and you could lose your life.* Even in modern contexts, infidelity can be costly.
- ➢ Even today in some countries such as Iran and Afghanistan, adultery is punishable by death, often by stoning, though the "offenders" are usually women.

In most modern societies, unfaithfulness is rewarded with impunity and approval rather than severe punishment. However, it's an undeniable fact that moral failure unleashes disastrous effects on human lives. In the Christian context, the cost can be enormous, especially when it happens in the lives of leaders. And we must ask:

What is the damage that is done? *Who* are the ones affected? And *how* are they affected?

Damage Occasioned by a Moral Fall

The Loss of Ministry

In many cases of moral impropriety, a person is removed from a ministry or leadership position. This is a huge loss, accompanied by humiliation, emotional devastation, economic crises and other difficulties. The disobedience of King Saul cost him his kingdom.[25] For his indulgence in immorality, Samson lost his sight, his liberty, his strength, his dignity, and the further opportunity of being Israel's liberator. The Bible warns, "For a harlot is a deep pit, and a seductress is a narrow well" (Proverbs 23:27). The NIV says, "For an adulterous woman is a deep pit, and a wayward wife is a narrow well."

Thomas is an example. Pastor of a large church in a Latin American country, he permitted his romantic attraction to a woman in his church to grow until it culminated in a liaison. Attempts at restoration were made by his overseers, but he was unwilling to confront and conquer the hang-ups and character flaws in his life. Finally, Thomas aborted the restoration process and left the church.

> *In many cases of a moral fall, a person is removed from their ministry.*

Cases abound of pastors who have lost their churches and ministries and of missionaries and other leaders who have been removed

---

[25] The sin of Saul was not sexual but nonetheless involved disobedience to the clear directives of God, triggering the high cost of his sin: the loss of his kingdom. First Samuel 26:21 records his pathetic words, "Indeed I have played the fool and erred exceedingly." Saul is a prototype of leaders and believers in general who suffer great loss due to lack of discipline in turning from their sin and repenting.

from ministry. Some regain the capacity to resume a leadership role, while others battle for years to reconstruct their life and ministry from the ashes and rubble of their fall.[26] Pastors Ricardo and Jonathan, mentioned in chapter 1, lost their ministries as well as their families.

Sam was a popular conference speaker who headed a para-church ministry to couples through seminars and similar events. After being married for many years and teaching thousands of couples on successful marriage, he made the disastrous decision to divorce his wife—whom he said he never loved—and married a woman much younger than he. His ministry descended in a nosedive and disappeared.

The pastor of a church of 1,200 members carried on two and then three affairs simultaneously. His loss? Three hundred members for *each* of the three affairs. Since—unfortunately—he has no spiritual covering to intervene, he continues to pastor, but now his flock consists of only three hundred, one-fourth its former size.

Shame

Fallen pastors have wept bitterly on my shoulder as I embraced them. Some have begged, "Please don't tell other pastors or my church!" The psalmist says, "Oh, that my ways were steadfast in obeying your decrees! Then I would not be put to shame when I consider all your commands" (119:5–6, NIV). All too often this lament is expressed when it is too late.

Proverbs 6:23–28, 32–33 delivers a solemn message to those who play with the fire of illicit sex. Although a little long, it's worth reading thoughtfully.

---

[26] This is not to say that permanent loss of ministry happens in all cases. Although some scholars and Bible teachers take the position that a fallen pastor can never return to pastoral ministry, many believe such restoration is possible—at least in some cases—and should be the goal. I recognize that in some cases restoration is complicated and aborted by bad attitudes, lack of true repentance and willingness to change on the part of the fallen person. True genuine repentance is a prerequisite for any restoration to be successful.

> For the commandment is a lamp, And the law a light; Reproofs of instruction are the way of life, To keep you from the evil woman, From the flattering tongue of a seductress. Do not lust after her beauty in your heart, Nor let her allure you with her eyelids. For by means of a harlot [promiscuous woman] a man is reduced to a crust of bread; And an adulteress will prey upon his precious life. Can a man take fire to his bosom, And his clothes not be burned? Can one walk on hot coals, And his feet not be seared? So is he who goes in to his neighbor's wife; Whoever touches her shall not be innocent. (6:23–28, author's note)
>
> Whoever commits adultery with a woman lacks understanding; He who does so destroys his own soul. Wounds and dishonor he will get, And his reproach will not be wiped away. (32–33)

Disobedience produces shame, which is, according to the dictionary, a painful emotion caused by guilt, dishonor, condemnation, ignominy, or disgrace.

James was a recognized leader, author, and pastor. His infidelity was discovered by a leader in his church who found a love note written to a woman of the congregation. At the end of a meeting with his group of elders, who confronted him, James left with the sting of shame burning in his heart. Calling his wife to pick him up, he fell, in a fetal position, in a dark hallway of the church, crying.

> *Pastors have wept on my shoulder, begging me not to tell.*

THE HIGH COST OF SEXUAL SIN

Spiritual and Emotional Storms

In Psalm 6:1–6 and Psalms 32 and 51, we can hear the groans of David under the discipline of God, suffering the effects of the storm that buffeted his soul. Guilt, depression, anger, fear, blame shifting, confusion, and hate are almost always the fruit of illicit sex. In addition to the hurricane assaulting the fallen person, the spouse has his or her own monsoon to weather. These emotional and spiritual upheavals consist of the following:

- *Guilt.* Unless their consciences are seared, fallen leaders will feel tremendous guilt, knowing they have violated God's Word and their wedding vows, have betrayed their biblical value system, and have sinned against God and others. At times, a wife feels guilty, believing she "has not supplied her husband's needs" or "been a good wife." The wife of a fallen minister said, "I feel I'm to blame for all this."
- *Depression.* The sense of desperation fallen persons feel causes them to ask, "Is there a way out of this? When will this storm pass? Will I lose my ministry, my salary? How will we live? Is there any hope of restoration from this? How will I face my children, my colleagues?" And other questions seem to have no immediate answer and plunge one into despondency.
- Depression is defined as "a mental condition of semidarkness and sadness, or dejection." It's discouragement and a sense of hopelessness, of seeing no way out. Self-esteem hits the floor. The wife of a fallen church leader lamented, "I feel so depressed."
- *Anger.* Persons trapped in illicit sex often feel anger toward themselves, for allowing the situation to occur. Their anger may cause them to shift the blame to their spouse. Or maybe the paramour is the target of their anger, for revealing the affair or breaking off the relationship. Or perhaps it's the whistleblower, the person who discovered and dis-

closed the secret. Anger may even be directed at God, who "engineered" the disclosure and didn't allow them to enjoy what they believe they "deserved and needed." Anger is a feeling of hostility, indignation, or exasperation. At times, anger is accompanied by the desire for revenge, to punish the one guilty of the perceived wrong.

➤ *Fear.* A person caught in the web of sexual sin, especially in an affair, lives in the shadow of fear. Fear of discovery, fear of consequences, such as losing his ministry, his livelihood, his marriage and family, his character and reputation. Or perhaps fear of blackmail.

> *A person caught in the web of sexual sin lives in the shadow of fear.*

➤ *Confusion.* The wife of a fallen pastor commented on the deep sense of confusion she felt upon learning of her husband's problem. "I didn't know what to expect or what to do." The fallen one likewise feels a dark cloud of confusion over his mind, removing, in some cases, the ability to think rationally. The person feels trapped and sees no way out of the abyss. Clear decisions elude him as he struggles with the choice of whether or not to confess his sin and abort destructive actions and relationships. He may try to convince himself that what he's doing isn't so bad, when in his heart of hearts he knows his actions are sanctioned by the Bible and God's moral law. He knows he should abort and confess his illicit behavior but doesn't find in himself the strength of will and courage to do so.

➤ *Hatred.* At times, the torrid "love" they thought they held for the new flame turns to hatred, especially if that flame is the one who revealed their secret. One feels betrayed, and "love" becomes disdain and contempt. In 2 Samuel 13, we find a prime example:

THE HIGH COST OF SEXUAL SIN

"Amnon son of David fell in love with Tamar, the beautiful sister of Absalom" (2 Samuel 13:1, NIV). Through a series of tricks and deceit, Amnon seduced and raped her. After saying he was madly in love with her and tasting of the forbidden fruit, his "love" turned to enmity and aversion. Verse 15 says, "Then Amnon hated her exceedingly, so that the hatred with which he hated her *was* greater than the love with which he had loved her. And Amnon said to her, 'Arise, be gone!'"

One of the effects of illicit "love" is that it turns sour in the end. Forbidden fruit is sweet in the mouth but bitter in the stomach. What starts as sweetness ends as acerbity. Love turns to hate, which at times is followed by blackmail, demands of hush money, or character assassination. The "sweetness" turns to bitterness. The "flame" goes out and is now only smoke.

Character Damage

Something happens in the character of persons trapped in illicit sex. Immoral behavior begets other sins such as leading a double life, lying, disloyalty, deception, hypocrisy, manipulation, and betrayal.

These flaws, if recognized and corrected in time, can save us from becoming moral wreckage. If not, our character and testimony will suffer damage. Joyce Meyers says that our character is formed by many acts but can be shattered by a single act. That is true. Our reputation can be damaged by others, but only we can tarnish our character.

> *Our reputation can be damaged by others, but only we can damage our character.*

Trust Destroyed

As leaders, a good number of people place confidence in us, including our spouse, children, other leaders, friends, the congregation we attend or lead, and even the community in which we live. These persons believe we will set a good example, will hold high the biblical norms of uncorrupt living, and will fulfill their expectations of honesty and integrity. They want to be able to say with pride, "That's my spouse or my dad or my pastor or my teacher or my friend." When they discover we're not trustworthy, their confidence in us withers, like an unwatered plant in a south Texas sun.

Trust is the foundation of all human relationships. Once betrayed, trust is difficult to regain. We have to start anew to prove ourselves worthy of confidence that people can deposit in us in the future. This is especially true for a betrayed spouse.

Captivity

Part of the high cost of sexual sin is the sense of bondage, of being caught in a trap. We can become addicts of certain practices, victims of blackmail, or prisoners of our own lust. One man admitted, "I was freed from alcoholism in a moment, but my victory over pornography cost me four years of fierce struggle."[27]

Soul ties can ensnare us. When there is sexual intimacy between two persons, an emotional bond is formed that does not easily dissolve, even when the relations stop. God designed this for marriage, to strengthen the emotional and spiritual bond between husband and wife. When practiced outside marriage, the principle holds true: a strong bond is formed that emotionally "ties" one to the other in the soul realm. In 1 Corinthians 6:16, Paul says this "one flesh" tie can result even in the case of a harlot: "Do you not know that he who is joined to a harlot is one body with her? For 'The two,' He says, 'shall become one flesh.'" A church leader had intimate relations with a young girl from his church. Later, when her family moved far away

---

[27] Ted Roberts, *Pastors at Greater Risk* (Regal Books, 2003), 251.

to another state, the leader still felt an intense longing to be with her. Needless to say, this kind of situation has repeated itself many times, in many places, in many broken lives.

Venereal Diseases

When Albert, an active leader in his church, began to neglect his marriage and personal relationship with God, he had a series of affairs, the upshot of which was a venereal disease, which he transmitted to his wife. She had to undergo special treatments and surgery before becoming free of the malady.

> *We can become addicts of certain practices, victims of blackmail, or prisoners of our own lust.*

Experts tell us that when one has sexual relations with a person, he is having relations with all the persons that that person has had sex with in the last ten years. Author and counselor Jerry Kirk states: "Thus, in that sense, a man brings to his marriage bed any woman with whom he has had sex. This of course affects his ability to fully love his wife and enjoy with her a true and unique intimacy."[28] It's not unusual in this case to have mental images of past experiences with other partners, even during intimate times with one's spouse. This is besides any physical damage brought home from other "lovers."

We Wound Ourselves and Others

It is a grave error to think our life is ours to live as we want, or that our body is ours to do with it according to our desires and whims. The Bible says: "For none of us lives to himself, and no one

---

[28] Jerry Kirk, *Seven Promises of a Promise Keeper*, Focus on the Family (Colorado Springs, Colorado, 1994), 97.

dies to himself" (Romans 14:7). Our decisions and actions affect others. We have not been granted the right to live selfishly and for our own benefit and pleasure. We're responsible to live so that our life does not injure, but rather edifies, others. When we opt for a sinful lifestyle, we should remind ourselves that others *will* suffer. Who are the affected ones?

- **God.** We wound the heart of our heavenly Father when we disobey his commands, which are for our good. Proverbs 10:1 teaches us that, "A wise son makes a glad father, but a foolish son is the grief of his mother." The desire of all God's children should be to bring joy to His heart. Living in obedience is the only way and makes it possible for Him to say of us, as He did of Jesus, "This is my beloved son, in whom I am well pleased."
- **The Spouse.** Few wounds are as deep and cruel as spousal rejection. A wife gives away her life, her heart, her body, and her future to a man who promises to love, protect, and be faithful to her for life. The unfaithfulness of her husband says to her: "You no longer please me. I need something more. You are not what I need or want. You no longer supply my needs." The wife feels used, deceived, rejected, and betrayed.

> *The unfaithfulness of her husband says: "You no longer please me. I need something more.*

Consider the price Juanita, a pastor's wife, was forced to pay for her husband's disloyalty: When he had relations with a minor from his church, his action became known to news agencies, and he was soon arrested and incarcerated. Juanita was rejected by her church due to the stigma involved. Left without financial support, she was unable to make payments on the house and was forced to sell that along with some personal possessions. She ended up in a small apartment with her children. Also, because of the misdemeanor of her husband, the family of the girl sued the denomination of which the church was part. It was an enormous price to pay for a misdeed caused by uncontrolled lust.

When we marry, we promise to protect the heart of our mate—not break it! A woman whose heart was being examined by her doctor asked, "Does it sound broken?" When the great *Physician* examines the hearts of His people, does He find many of them broken? "In my forty-five years of counseling I have discovered that nothing causes more pain in a relationship than infidelity," states pastor and writer Tim Lahaye.[29]

- **Children.** The wife of a fallen pastor said, "One morning, after my husband resigned the church and left to go live with another woman, my little daughter was crying nonstop. I told her she had to be strong, and she replied, 'Mama, my strong is broken.'" Our children suffer the consequences of our wrongdoing, as witnessed in the greed and disobedience of Achan (Joshua 7) and the rebellion of Korah, Dathan, and Abiram (Numbers 16), whose families suffered punishment along with their familial heads.
- **Colleagues.** Fellow leaders typically lose confidence in a fallen shepherd and often must help carry the stigma and damaged testimony of the ministry or church involved. The example of the failed person nosedives, and positive influence is lost. Other leaders must work overtime, repairing damage, counseling persons wounded by the misdeed, and doing the work of the fallen person. Some invest much time, resources, and energy attempting to restore them.
- **Followers.** Often, people are wounded and disillusioned by the misconduct of leaders. Such leaders betray the trust of

---

[29] Tim Lahaye, *The Act of Marriage After 40* (Grand Rapids, Michigan: Zondervan Publishing House), 16.

their people, producing in them great discouragement and causing some to lose hope and turn away from the faith.

Some years ago, it fell our lot to help a church in the United States that had weathered a time of fierce turbulence, occasioned by ill-fitted and inept leadership. After much conflict, the former pastor had resigned and left. People who remained after the storm had lost faith in ministers and church leaders. Long-standing members were leaving the church, disillusioned. After several months of restorative ministry, God brought healing and fresh vision. Following the setting in of a new pastor, we saw the church return to its former strength and blessing. But here's the point: Afterward, some of the people told us, "You restored our faith in ministers and leaders, a confidence we had lost."

Restored credibility doesn't automatically happen. Always, misconduct leaves disenchanted and deeply wounded people in its wake. Our task as leaders is to heal the sheep, not injure them; to unite God's people, not scatter them; to bless our families, not bring a curse upon them.

- **We Ourselves.** We not only damage others, we injure ourselves in the process. Our character is sabotaged. We lose self-respect. Our self-esteem drops to below zero. Joy evaporates. We may work like slaves to "expiate" our sin. We feel like the hypocrites we've become. We compromise our values and convictions.

  Don was a youth pastor. From the age of eleven, he had been a captive of pornography. Now, as youth leader, he became sexually involved with a young girl of sixteen. (Sex with minors under eighteen is a crime in his country.) When his actions were revealed, he was arrested. Before his case was tried, Don took his own life—another instance of the destructive power and high cost of sexual sin.

- **Destroyed Friendships.** Due to the loss of trust, the lack of true repentance, bad attitudes, misunderstandings, and unwise decisions on the part of the fallen person, friendships that were solid are washed away like sandcastles by the incoming tide. Sexual sin destroys or damages friendships.

People of principle find it difficult to walk in close fellowship with persons who don't practice integrity and refuse to recognize and abandon their immoral conduct (see 1 Corinthians 5:9–11). This doesn't mean, of course, that we don't try to help restore a sinning brother or sister when there is true repentance and desire to be redeemed (see Galations 6:1–2). Unfortunately, not all cases end in restoration, as when the fallen person persists in wrong attitudes and refusal of the restoration process. In these cases, many friendships suffer shipwreck and sink in a sea of frustration and even enmity.

Lost Opportunities

As I related before, Samson lost the opportunity to liberate his people from the Philistines, glorify God before the watching world, be an example to the youths of Israel, and live a life of joy and accomplishment. He was a prisoner, not so much of the Philistines, as of his own lust. A pastor who fell into the trap of adultery said, "How many persons are wounded and how many souls will not be helped because of this adultery? It is a loss too great to bear!"

> *Samson was not so much a prisoner of the Philistines as of his own lust.*

How Much Does It Cost?

- What is the price of participating "in the unfruitful works of darkness?" (Ephesians 5:11) *Let's ask Samson:*

I was called to liberate Israel from the Philistines, and I began well. But the lust that controlled my life made me a slave rather than a liberator. Instead, I became a pathetic fool, an object of pity and ridicule, and the laughingstock of the Philistines.

- What is the price of sexual sin? *Let's ask David:*

    I killed bears, lions, and a giant. I led victorious armies that conquered enemies and expanded Israel's borders. I was king of Israel, psalmist, musician, poet, prophet. But I was conquered by the desires of the flesh, by my desire for the wife of another man, Uriah. I killed him, one of my most loyal and brave soldiers. I killed him to hide my sin and steal his wife. God forgave me, but I have had much suffering and chaos in my family. My son Amnon raped his half sister Tamar. Absalom killed Amnon, his brother, and led a rebellion against me that caused me much anguish before his bloody and shameful death. When I was dying, another son, Adonijah, tried to usurp the throne before the coronation of Solomon—my choice for king—could take place. I trust that in heaven "goodness and mercy shall follow me," but "all the days of my life" now are filled with pain since my tryst with Bathsheba. (See 2 Samuel 11–12; Psalms 32 and 51.)

- What is the cost of giving loose rein to carnality? *Let's ask Lot:*

    I wanted to reside in Sodom, for the economic benefits. Afterwards I saw it was a grave mistake. God pulled us out of there before destroying the city, but the atmosphere we lived in for years took its toll. My wife died because of disobedience. My two daughters committed incest with me, their father. Yes, I actually had sexual intimacy with my own daughters, although I didn't know it until later because I was drunk! And, as if this were not enough, two sons were born from them, Moab and Ben-ammi, progenitors of the Moabites and Amonites, peoples who later were a thorn in the flesh to Israel. First, I was a problem to Abraham, then to all Israel.

- How high is the price of disobedience of God's commands? *Let's ask Eli, the priest:*

    My sons, also priests, cheated by taking the best parts of the offerings brought to the tabernacle by the people. But worse, yes much worse, was their conduct with the women who served in the house of God: having sexual relations with them. And I tolerated such conduct. The price of all this? God cut off the priesthood from my descendants and me. I lost my ministry. My sons died in war, the Ark of the Covenant was captured by the Philistines, and I have nothing left to live for.

These are laments of Bible personages who succumbed to temptation. Along with the sad words of many contemporary believers and leaders, they are an eloquent testimony of the exorbitant cost of illicit sex.

The Great Rip-Off Artist

Sin is the great thief! It steals our ability to fulfill our ministries with joy and to finish our race with victory. It robs the true success God had planned for us. It rips us off of a happy marriage and family. It seizes our self-respect and the respect of others. It filches our time, health, and physical, mental, emotional, and spiritual strength. It hijacks our character, integrity, and trust and pilfers our anointing and dreams and destiny. This thief comes only "to steal, and to kill, and to destroy" (John 10:10). Pastor and counselor of ministers, H. B. London, Jr., said, "Infidelity...sabotages the work of God."[30]

Satan, with his devices, is the great thief. And what do we get in return for all we lose? Pain, anguish, depression, failure, unbearable burdens, confusion, shame, slavery, mirages, bitterness, empty promises, and disillusionment.

If the price of sin is so high, why are people willing to risk so much for so little, like trading a new, luxury car for a worn-out, dilapidated jalopy? Many, in many parts of the world, at this very moment, are walking on the slippery edge of a moral precipice or are like sheep being led to the slaughter. In the following chapter, we'll explore some of the reasons why.

For Reflection

1. If you are now practicing some sexual sin, have you considered the cost?
2. Do you believe the "reward" ("to enjoy the passing pleasures of sin," Hebrews 11:25) that Samson, David, Lot, and the sons of Eli received was of greater value than that given by God for obedience? Why?
3. Why do you think servants of God risk so much to receive so little in exchange?

---

[30] H. B. London, Jr., and Neil B. Wiseman, *Pastors at Greater Risk* (Regal Books, 2003), 50.

6

Under the Influence
Causes of Moral Failure

A curse without cause shall not alight.
—Proverbs 26:2b

Don't look at where you fell; look at where you slipped.
—Liberian proverb

Whathat influences contribute to a moral fall in the life of a leader, or any believer for that matter? No one factor alone proves a person is in sin, or in danger of a fall. But together they serve as indicators of the need for caution and vigilance, "lest Satan should take advantage of us; for we are not ignorant of his devices" (2 Corinthians 2:11). When any of these warning signs are present, the wise person will slow down and take inventory of what is happening in his or her life and make adjustments to avoid a disaster on a dangerous curve.

The descent into moral disarray has two phases. (1) The *preparation*: situations in our life, marriage or work, prepare us, that is, make us vulnerable to temptation. (2) The *opportunity*: when the situations prepare us, sooner or later the opportunity, the temptation, will present itself to us. In this chapter, we'll examine some of the *influences* (preparation) that can become *causes* of a slide into sexual sin.

Overloaded Agendas. A study of twenty-five pastors trapped in sexual sin revealed that 80 percent of them were addicted to their work—workaholics—overloaded with excess of activities and responsibilities. This is a frequent cause of trouble and affects in the following ways:

> *80 percent of the pastors were workaholics.*

- Physical and mental exhaustion rob us of the energy we should dedicate to our families.
- Excess of work absorbs the leader and drains off time needed for cultivating the marriage relationship. In one study of pastors, 80 percent said they do not share sufficient time with their spouse.[31] One leader expressed, "I've been an addict of my work in ministry, and it cost me my family. Recently my wife divorced me and left with our children. Now my life is lonely and empty." Christian psychologist James Dobson has stated that the overload of activities and work is the number one assassin of marriages.
- In many cases, the leader's wife works in the public domain or in ministry, which complicates the state of affairs because

---

[31] H. B. London, Jr., and Neil B. Wiseman, *Pastors at Greater Risk* (Regal Books, 2003), 86. Information taken originally from a survey with pastors by Focus on the Family.

she also struggles with scarcity of time and energy. One pastor commented, "The greatest need in our marriage is communication, tolerance, and patience. I feel my wife doesn't support me. We lack time to be together because we have different ministries, besides two small children and another on the way." It isn't difficult to understand the frustration of this pastor. He has no time to cultivate the marriage and neither does she. In these cases, love and companionship are like a campfire where no one is putting more wood on the flame. Result? It goes out.

- Fatigue and wear and tear of our work lower our guard and make resisting temptation more daunting. This "wearing down" is caused by problems in the ministry: conflicts with members or other leaders, administration, business meetings, counseling, and study ("much study is wearisome to the flesh," Ecclesiastes 12:12). Another study of pastoral life revealed that fully 40 percent of pastors experience a serious conflict with a church member at least once a month.[32]

> *Fatigue and wear and tear lower our guard and make resisting temptation more daunting.*

A Sense of Entitlement. Some justify improper conduct with the argument: "I work so hard and produce so much for the church that, really, I deserve a little joy and pleasure. I believe God understands." These deceptive thoughts can invade the mind of one who believes he is entitled to more than he is getting, especially if there is a propensity toward sexual sin.

Problems in the Leader's Marriage. The wife of a fallen leader expressed, "My husband's affair is not what was destroying our marriage. Our marriage is what was destroying our marriage!" That is, the terrible condition of the marriage was causing it to self-destruct.

---

[32] Ibíd., 20.

An affair is a symptom of a gloomy, failing marriage. One pastor lamented, "We need help to escape this vicious circle of attacking and doing destructive things to each other."

As I commented in chapter 1, 50 percent of pastors are not satisfied with their intimate life in their marriages. When this occurs, the trap of sexual sin has been set. Another leader confided, "I am afraid a 'fatal attraction' will present itself and will destroy my marriage."

Many leaders do not see the importance of cultivating their own marriage and home life. In a survey of pastors, only 12 percent said that their number one priority was their family.[33] Many need help and counseling. Forty-eight percent said that being in ministry is harmful to their family.[34]

Boredom. In many cases, a straying husband is bored with his marriage and the intimate life he no longer enjoys or is even bored with life itself. Or he may be weary of the unending routines and demands of ministry that make life tasteless, without refreshment or creativity. A new challenge is needed, and an affair offers to satisfy that "need" for something new and different. Of course, the same can be true of a wife.

> *An affair is a symptom of a gloomy, failing marriage.*

Often, instead of seeking renewal of the relationship and companionship within the marriage, a person looks outside for the solution. When we find ourselves in this mood, and a temptation appears in the form of an attractive person, it isn't easy to resist.

Lack of Caution in Opposite Sex Friendships. Many affairs sprout from this type of relationship. Frequent social contact between opposite sex friends is fertile ground for improper feelings to bud and blossom, whether individuals or couples. While there is nothing inherently wrong with the friendship itself, great

---
[33] Ibíd., 264.
[34] Ibíd., 86.

care must be taken to ensure we stay within proper boundaries. If we permit romantic feelings to exist and grow, the friendship could be headed toward shipwreck, like the ill-fated *Titanic*. Not only does the friendship sink, but it often takes marriages down with it. A friendship can become romanticized, and a romanticized friendship can easily become sexualized. A sad example is Ben and Nancy. Best friends of another couple, they frequently socialized and enjoyed each other's company. That is, until Ben began to have amorous feelings for his best friend's wife. It ended with Ben's adultery with his wife's best friend! Wise is the person—man or woman—who has drawn their boundary lines in advance.

Pride. I believe king David's fall with Bathsheba was not caused so much by lust as by pride: "I'm the king; I have power and authority; I can do what I want and have what I desire; and I desire that woman!"

Pride makes us feel we are superior to our mate and that we deserve more than he or she can give us. This attitude opens the door to temptation. "Pride goes before destruction, and a haughty spirit before a fall" (Proverbs 16:18). This is one of the signs God puts in our way to warn us of a dangerous curve ahead. Pride causes us to undervalue our spouse and overvalue ourselves; humility motivates us to appreciate and thank God for our mate.

In another chapter, I mentioned the Christian educator Howard Hendricks who carried a little notebook with more than a hundred names of known ministers and former students who had had a moral fall. He went on to report that all but two of them fell under the influence of pride and arrogance!

Low Self-Esteem. A person with a low self-image believes they are of little value, are unattractive, and have little talent or usefulness.

> *Those who don't know their worth, sell themselves cheap.*

The problem occurs when we seek our value in wrong places and in wrong ways. It's the culprit behind the fall into sexual immorality of many young girls. If they had a healthier concept of their value as persons, they would not be easy prey for predators who desire to use them to satisfy their lust. We must know that our worth is founded on the love God has for us as worthy persons. Those who know their value to God will not easily fall into the sexual sin trap. They understand they are made in the image of God and are precious to Him. Those who don't know their worth sell themselves cheap.

Pastors and leaders are not exempt from battles with low self-esteem. A survey revealed that 70 percent suffer from a lower self-image than when they began their ministries.[35] Also, half of the pastors surveyed said they don't feel competent to face the demands of pastoral ministry.[36]

Loneliness. A medical missionary in South America was away from his home much of the time, visiting villages and curing the sick. His wife was unable to accompany him on his travels and, with time, began to feel the acute and constant loneliness created by his absences. Her friendship with a man from the community began to blossom and distended into episodes of adultery with him.

> *She felt unable to resist the hunger for affection created by her absentee husband's inattention.*

Conquered by loneliness, she felt unable to resist the hunger for affection created by her absentee husband's inattention. Loneliness in a marriage is another of the dangerous curves on the highway of life. Unfortunately, neither she nor her husband gave heed to the warning signs in time.

---

[35] Ibíd., 172.
[36] Ibíd., 20.

Many affairs begin not in a search for the sexual factor or even of romance but as an escape from loneliness. One counselor believes it is three times more likely for an affair to occur as the result of a search for companionship than for romance or sex. The problem is that the relationship seldom remains on that level but progresses toward the romantic and sexual. Dennis Rainey, another expert in counseling, author, and Bible teacher, said, "I have never counseled a person whose affair began on a sexual note, but rather an emotional one."[37]

A wife, starved for conversation with her unusually quiet husband, one day greeted her neighbor over the fence of their yard. He showed interest in her, asking questions and conversing. Another day they chatted again, and she began to feel her heart responding to his attention and consideration of her. This person felt she had value, while her husband almost never conversed with or showed interest in her. Drawn by the new joy and attraction of the neighbor, she eventually lost her battle with temptation. This tragedy could have been avoided if the wife had guarded her heart more carefully (Proverbs 4:23) and if the husband had read the signs and cared for his wife and marriage. A search for communication and companionship ended in marital unfaithfulness.

Neglect of Our Personal Relationship with God. The well-known educator, Howard Hendricks, did a survey with six hundred fallen pastors. His report showed that almost all had three things in common:

1) Lack of time spent in personal communion with God.
2) No accountability with anyone.
3) Almost all thought: "That will never happen to me."

When we neglect our communion with the Lord, a door is opened, admitting influences that alienate us from Him. When we are not close to Him, we cannot hear His voice clearly. Our heart

---

[37] Dennis Rainey. Recorded interview with Tom Eisenman, a resource produced by Family Life Today, Little Rock, Arkansas

becomes cold, and our attitudes are not malleable. We don't think biblically, with God's thoughts. Our vision blurs. We lose our sense of direction and purpose. Our service to God becomes mechanical and routine. Spiritual passion fades. And what does all this produce? A prime candidate for a fall. Carelessness in communion with God is a foreshadowing of "Danger Ahead."

> *When we neglect communion with God, a door is opened, admitting influences that alienate us from Him.*

The Revenge Affair. Another motive behind moral failure is the desire to get even when a spouse has been unfaithful. The offended one decides that the best way to do that, to castigate the offender, is to have their own affair, thus paying the spouse back in their own coin. Rather than fixing the problem, it confounds it. Unfortunately, this happens even among spiritual leaders.

The Lure of the Affair. The spirit of adventure, of exploring new territories, of a new challenge, of conquering another mountain, pulls at the heart of many persons, especially where there is boredom with their present state. (In Spanish, the same word is used for *adventure* and *affair*.) An affair offers the opportunity to discover new pleasures, to be allured to new experiences. The fact that they are censored makes them even more enticing and intriguing, since forbidden fruit has a special fascination and appeal. Satan offered new experiences, new knowledge, and new power to Adam and Eve. His attractive promise made them believe the risk would be minimal compared with the "reward." The problem was that the promise was a deception, and the reward turned to punishment, pain, and loss.

The Confused Role of a Wife. In one case of adultery, the straying husband gave this reason for his affair: His wife assumed the role of mother. He stated, "I don't want my wife to treat me like a child that needs his mother's care. I want her in the role of my lover, not my mother." In another case, a doctor divorced his wife and married his assistant who was much less attractive than his wife. When asked why, he said, "My wife treated me like a son. This woman treats me like the man that I am." Every man who is a man needs a woman who will treat him as such.

Unmet Needs. As mentioned previously, two things work in tandem to push a person into an affair or other forms of sexual aberration: preparation and opportunity. One thing that prepares is unmet emotional and sexual needs. We feel frustrated and become vulnerable to temptation. The second element is a situation or person (the opportunity) that offers to meet needs not being met in legitimate ways. When a person has been prepared, the opportunity will not be long in coming. Sin is the attempt to satisfy legitimate needs in illegitimate ways.

> *When the person has been prepared, the opportunity will not be long in coming.*

Society and Culture Saturated with Sex. Almost every day we are bombarded with material of a seductive and sexual flavor on billboards, TV, magazines, cinema, Internet, and other media. Society's norms differ greatly from the Bible's standards. By society's moral code, it is acceptable (and in some cases, expected) to have a lover in addition to the spouse.

> *Sin is the attempt to satisfy legitimate needs in illegitimate ways.*

Open marriage—the mutually-agreed-upon liberty to enjoy sexual escapades with others—is cool to some. In our sexually charged culture, almost anything goes. Some television shows promote immorality and adultery. Divorce is an easy way out of a marriage gone sour. Others cohabit, not bothering with the "inconvenience" of marriage. A Christian who worked in an office with twenty-three other women said that she was the only one who was faithful to her husband! And the others jibed her, asking: "What's your problem?" To them, marital faithfulness was a "problem." To live by biblical standards in societies and cultures saturated with sex is like Joseph living in purity in the house of Potiphar or Daniel in Babylon. Those two spiritual giants proved that it is possible to live in moral purity even in that kind of atmosphere. So can we, but we must measure our conduct and live by God's rules and not the current culture's yardstick.

Delilah and Jezebel Are Not Dead. There is one more cause worthy of mention: available women, single, divorced, widowed (or married!) who seek the companionship of a man and have no scruples about how to attract one. Such situations appear in the workplace, in public places, even in church. Their way of dressing, talking, and flirting is designed to attract a vulnerable partner. Some have a "relationship addiction," bouncing from one relationship to another. One young lady I know, desperate to marry, became an easy conquest for the young man she desired. Her scheme worked, and she won her prize when she became pregnant and he married her. Another woman brazenly stated, "I use sex to get what I want!" All of the Delilahs and Jezebels and Potiphar's wives are not dead. Some are still around in the twenty-first century. Of course, often the tables are turned, and the man is in the role of predator.

> *"What really matters is me, my happiness, in spite of pain it produces in others."*

These are some of the more common causes of a descent into the abyss of illicit sex. Their presence indicates we may be on a dangerous curve and need to slow down and evaluate our situation. When more than one is obvious, it's a red flag that shouts: Danger Ahead. Stop! If you are living under the influence of any of these possible causes of a moral collapse, look to the infallible moral code, which teaches "us that, denying ungodliness and worldly lusts, we should live soberly, righteously, and godly in the present age" (Titus 2:12). Only then can we navigate the dangerous curves successfully.

For Reflection

1. Are you aware of any of these influences in your life that might cause a tendency to yield to moral temptation?
2. What is the present condition of your marriage? (if married) Are there areas such as communication, intimate life, compatibility, etc. that need strengthening? Is there boredom or other factors that could make you a candidate for a moral fall?
3. How are you handling the balance between your presence and absence at home (the pressures of work versus the need for quality time with your spouse?)
4. How is your personal relationship with God? Is there negligence or diligence in keeping your spiritual life strong?
5. What are some things that prepare us for a fall, and what are some examples of "opportunities" that present temptations?

7

Warning Signs
God's Early Warning System

A prudent man sees danger and takes refuge, but the simple keep going and suffer for it.

—Proverbs 22:3

Several years ago, my wife, Annis, and I were traveling by car in Canada. Suddenly a man with a red flag signaled us to stop, warning us that a bridge had collapsed ahead. He also told us that the day before a driver paid no attention to the warning and speeded on. His vehicle plunged into the open space killing two persons. We thanked God for the man and his warning sign.

The words of Solomon (cited above) describe the contrast between a wise person who heeds warnings and a foolish one who doesn't:

- ➢ He who heeds warnings is *prudent*. He who does not is *simple*. Some translations render it *simpleton*.
- ➢ The prudent one *sees*, has his eyes open, scanning for possible hazards. He is a person who discerns, thinks, and stays alert. His head is in neither the clouds nor the sand. "Be sober, be vigilant; because your adversary the devil walks about like a roaring lion, seeking whom he may devour" (1 Peter 5:8).

> *He is a person who discerns,*
> *thinks, and stays alert.*

- ➢ The judicious person, the *prudent* one, recognizes the danger and *hides himself* and *takes refuge*. He anticipates and avoids the traps and questionable situations.
- ➢ The simple one *passes on* and *keeps going*, speeds ahead to where there is no bridge. Such folly is based on lies, myths, and false beliefs that deceive the simple one: "Others have fallen but you won't. Others have suffered but not you. Others were caught but you won't be. You deserve this." He lives in an imaginary world that says, "Everything is fine and under control." He floats in a bubble he believes will never burst.
- ➢ Finally, Proverbs 22:3 teaches us that the simple *do* "suffer for it" and will be "punished." The NLT says, "A prudent person foresees danger and takes precautions. The simpleton goes blindly on and suffers the consequences." There *are* consequences, punishment, and suffering waiting ahead, inevitably and inescapably. The only sane con-

clusion is a determination to heed the signs and avoid the pitfalls. But what are those signs?

What Are the Signs?

Although here I speak from a man's perspective, women also experience sexual temptation, and each warning can apply to the feminine sex as well. Infidelity may be more common among men than women, but no one is immune from temptation.

Not only should each person be aware of warning signs but also warnings from others, such as a spouse, friends, colleagues, or even one's children. These can be of help in detecting when a potential problem is brewing. In one case, a group of intercessors in a church had a persisting impression that their pastor was at risk in his moral life. Numerous times they spoke to him, and each time he denied there was a problem. Not long afterward, his adultery was exposed, and he suffered grave consequences, attempting to cross where there was no bridge. While living in Costa Rica, I considered hiring Sandra, a young married woman as secretary. My wife, Annis, felt uneasy about that arrangement, and I desisted from the decision. Afterward, we discovered Sandra's marriage was on the rocks, and later she was divorced. I was glad I listened to my wife and avoided what could have been a dangerous curve.

- ***The other woman has problems in her marriage.*** A pastor or leader who counsels women with problems in their marriages should be especially cautious. This area can be a minefield.

    A woman in this case probably has needs her husband is not supplying, such as a lack of affection, loving and caring attention, etc. She can be vulnerable to attention received from the counselor, and she can misinterpret his actions. In some counseling situations, a counselee can begin to believe the counselor not only has the answer but *is* the answer to her problem.

> *A counselee can begin to believe the counselor not only has the answer but is the answer to her problem.*

Apart from counseling, there are times when a man with a listening ear and understanding heart can sympathize with a female coworker or neighbor whose marriage is on the rocks and end up being the answer to her dilemma.

- **Your own marriage has problems.** Of course, this can work both ways: the man being the one looking for a listening ear and a shoulder on which to find refuge from a shipwrecked relationship. It is he who now has a vacuum in his life and needs someone to fill it.

  When both the man (counselor) and the woman (counselee) have troubled marriages, it becomes a minefield, doubly dangerous. Each is vulnerable because they "understand each other," share their "pain," have the same needs, and begin to mutually satisfy those needs. In another chapter, I will offer suggestions for avoiding these and similar situations.

- **The other woman meets needs in your life the spouse does not fill.** This is similar to the last point, but it can occur in any kind of situation. And when it happens, in or out of the counseling arena, it's an alert that merits special attention.

  Characteristics of the sign: You feel happy, joyful, fulfilled, and upbeat for the first time in a long time. Her words inspire you and lift your spirits. You feel a new energy and motivation. Her company pleases and fills you with delight. She is meeting your needs for affection, respect, and intimacy. All this is a sign that your emotions are out of control and you are on a dangerous curve.

- ***There's a strong desire to be with her.*** The woman seeks to be near you and you to her. You invent excuses and occasions to be together. If the two of you work together, such opportunities may abound. Thoughts of her fill your mind, and the desire to be together is mutual. You look forward to the next rendezvous with joy and excitement. The desire to be together, to talk, to touch, is meeting a need in you and in her.

> *The desire to be together, to talk, to touch, is meeting a need in you and in her.*

- ***You begin to justify and excuse your feelings, actions, and attitudes.*** When we know we are doing something wrong but want to continue, the mind searches for ways to justify the action. Rationalization is a key trick of the mind to accomplish it. "After all, you deserve it." "Your mate doesn't understand you and your needs." "It's not all that wrong." One man told me, "We didn't take all our clothes off." Another: "I kept my wedding ring on the whole time." Rationalizations are simply thoughts that need to be "brought into captivity to the obedience of Christ" (2 Corinthians 10:5). Translation: every wrong or impure thought must submit and become obedient to Christ. That is done by "casting down arguments and every high thing that exalts itself against the knowledge of God." Translation: all arguments and supposedly intellectual reasoning in disagreement with God must be cast down, like the demolition of an old building.
- ***You begin to lie, deceive, and cover up.*** Not only do you rationalize your behavior, but now you resort to a darker area: falsehood and hypocrisy. Every effort is made at hiding behavior, covering your tracks, painting over one lie with another, anything to avoid discovery. If you persist in this

behavior long enough, you not only lie, you become a liar; you not only practice hypocrisy, you become a hypocrite; you not only deceive, you become a deceiver; you not only commit adultery, you become an adulterer. Now, it's not just something you do, it's something you have become.

- ***Warnings from the spouse.*** I mentioned above how others can help us detect when a problem is evincing in our life. A wife's help is invaluable since she has been given special radar to discern trouble areas. When she senses that a problem is in the making, it's because that spiritual radar is setting off a warning. What is often interpreted as jealousy is something God placed in a woman for the protection of her marriage. It is normal for her to express her concerns, and it is normal for her husband to accuse her of being overly jealous. Just as a wife may warn her husband of a danger in travel, she can advise him of a spiritual or moral hazard. Her inquietudes can be a signal that a tempted husband should take seriously. God may use her concerns to save her husband from a moral disaster.

- ***Direct warnings from God.*** The Holy Spirit brings restraints in our spirit to warn us of moral danger lurking in the shadows ahead. Our conscience also warns us of wrong actions, urging prudence in our conduct. The reading of the Bible sheds light on God's expectations of us: "The entrance of Your words gives light; It gives understanding to the simple" (Psalm 119:130). When we read Scripture, God speaks to us. Meditating on such texts as Proverbs 5, 6, and 7; 1 Thessalonians 4:3–8; 1 Corinthians 6; 1 Timothy 4:12, 5:22b; 2 Timothy 2:22; Hebrews 13:4; and Ephesians 5 helps keep us on track spiritually. God's Word has a cleansing effect on our souls and serves to warn, illuminate, purify, and encourage us (Jeremiah 15:16, John 15:3). Wise is the person who heeds its admonitory message. Obedience to God's voice produces peace, righteousness, and blessing. Disobedience begets pain, loss, and regret.

Reading and Heeding
Why Do We Ignore the Signs?

Why do we, in spite of flashing lights and wide-open eyes, rush and stumble headlong into a trap? I believe there are several reasons why we humans disregard warning signs. Here are a few of them.

- We believe "that could never happen to me." We even deny we have a problem when we patently do! We think we are immune. We believe we are *fall-proof*. "Let him who thinks he stands take heed lest he fall" (1 Corinthians 10:12). Overconfident Peter learned the hard way: "I'll never deny you, Lord. These other guys might, but me, never!" We believe the warning signs were put there for the other guy, not for us.

> *We believe the warning signs were put there for the other guy, not for us.*

- We believe there's much ado about signs. "They're not really as serious a deal as some seem to think. Other people are not as skillful in driving as I am. My great ability allows me to navigate dangerous curves and take risks too hazardous for others." This thought occurred to every driver represented by a little cross beside a highway somewhere. And it lodges in the mind of every believer and servant of God that daringly accelerates toward a moral catastrophe.

This overdose of self-confidence in our ability to successfully handle any situation reminds one of Jeremiah 17:5–6,

> Cursed is the man who trusts in man and makes flesh his strength, whose heart departs from the Lord. For he shall be like a shrub in the desert, and shall not see when good comes, but shall inhabit the parched places in the wilderness.

Too many believers now dwell in "parched places in the wilderness" and in the ruins of a prosperous ministry and a marriage that once enjoyed the blessing of God.

- Spiritual and emotional immaturity. Children and adolescents rarely recognize the danger of drugs, liquor, immorality, driving without a license, etc. God gives us parents or guardians to protect us until we mature and become capable of making sensible and wise decisions.

The problem arises when there's a thirteen-year-old mind in a forty-year-old body. Thoughts, reactions, and decisions will not be adequate to meet the challenges of temptation. The benumbing power of temptation robs the brain's ability to think rationally and count the cost of an imprudent decision. A comedian cleverly commented that God gave man a brain and a masculine organ but not enough blood for both to function at the same time!

> *We believe we can easily handle any problem that arises.*

- Needs justify the risk. We believe our needs justify risky decisions and actions. We play the "My wife doesn't understand me, I deserve some fresh air, a change of scenery, I work so hard and deserve it" game. Caution is thrown to the wind in light of our pressing *neediness*. What is this but malodorous arrogance and noxious selfishness? *"My needs trump my wife's needs and the call to work together to* make the marriage work. *My needs* justify any risk I think necessary."

"Let nothing be done through selfish ambition or conceit, but in lowliness of mind let each esteem others better than himself. Let each of you look out not only for his own interests, but also for the interests of others." (Philippians 2:3–4)

- The euphoria experienced during an affair (or other sexual aberrations) blinds one to warnings—the ecstasy, the delight, the pleasure, the bliss produce a kind of intoxication. Until his world comes crashing down with a discovery of the sin (and it will!), he will believe the advantages outweigh the risks. Or he tells himself that this will be the last time, knowing it won't be.

Whatever the reason for showing indifference to the signs, it is risky business and exposes us to the danger of serious consequences to life and ministry. Not reading and heeding the warnings can be catastrophic.

The Price of Lack of Vigilance

December 7, 1941, began as a quiet, peaceful Sunday morning at Pearl Harbor Naval Base in Hawaii. Personnel carried on normal activities. Radar operators saw some suspicious signs on screen but paid little attention since everything was "normal." A few hours later, at 7:55 a.m., wave after wave of nearly two hundred Japanese bombers descended on the fleet of navy ships and the adjoining military base. A great number of US planes and ships were destroyed, and some 2,300 navy personnel were killed.

All was in a state of total unpreparedness. The reason? Radar operators, whose job it was to sound warnings of danger, attributed no importance to signs of approaching peril. Hundreds of lives could have been saved by the simple act of reading and heeding the signs. The catastrophe was not unavoidable. Warnings were present and obvious; lack of vigilance spawned the tragedy. Heedlessness can cause us to pay a very high price.

> *Heedlessness can cause us to pay a very high price.*

Negligence can unleash moral catastrophes in our lives, and it carries a pricey tab. Hundreds—perhaps thousands—of ministries, churches, lives, and marriages could have been saved by heeding warnings that were evident, conspicuous, and arresting. For some the bombs have fallen, the damage is done, and vigilance must turn to restoration. But for thousands more who are being lured by temptation's magnetic pull, there is time to heed signs and, by exercising vigilance now, avoid painful consequences. God patiently allows us time to repent and change course. We do not have to be charmed by the "fatal attraction" of an affair or immoral act. Like the prodigal we can look around, see the signs, count the cost, heed the warnings, make a life-transforming decision, and come home to a life of moral purity.

For Reflection

1. Do you see warning signs God puts in your way as a blessing or a bother? Why?
2. What do you believe is God's purpose for showing us the signs?
3. What should be our attitude as we observe the warnings?
4. How does being alert and prepared (before confronting a temptation) help us to overcome and be victorious over the enticement?

8

Myths and Lies We Believe: In Search of Truth

Do not be deceived.

—Galatians 6:7

The devil…does not stand in the truth, because there is no truth in him. When he speaks a lie, he speaks from his own resources, for he is a liar and the father of it.

—John 8:44

The most dangerous lies are those that resemble the truth. In times of temptation, the first casualty is truth.

MYTHS AND LIES WE BELIEVE: IN SEARCH OF TRUTH

The dictionary defines a myth as a fanciful, fictitious story, or half-truth. A good definition for our purpose is this: an assumption commonly believed, but untrue. By contrast, a lie is more blatant—a brassy untruth meant to deceive.

Satan, the Deceiver and Liar Par Excellence

Jesus revealed that Satan, our great enemy, not only is a liar, but the father (originator, source, author, fountainhead, root) of lies. All falsehood and deception have their origin in him (John 8:44). "So the great dragon was cast out, that serpent of old, called the Devil and Satan, who deceives the whole world; he was cast to the earth, and his angels were cast out with him" (Revelation 12:9).

> *Satan is not only a liar, but "the father of lies."*

In his rebellion against God (Isaiah 14:12–15, Ezekiel 28), he beguiled a third of the angels, who joined him in his insurrection (Revelation 12:4). Doubtless he promised them great authority and treasure—the scheme he attempted with Jesus, without success (Matthew 4:1–11)—but instead is leading them into the same abyss that is *his* final destination. Then he set about to deceive and destroy God's masterpiece, man.

In the garden, Satan succeeded in deceiving Eve with the lie that it is unnecessary to obey God, that there would be no consequences, only benefits. The act of disobedience drove humankind into spiritual ruin and separation from God (see Isaiah 59:1–2). Only the redemption that came through Christ can restore man from that moral waterloo and spiritual bankruptcy.

DANGEROUS CURVES

> *Disobedience drove humankind into spiritual ruin and separation from God.*

Our adversary has never stopped lying and deluding humanity. It has been said that the devil has two main objectives: (1) to keep people from trusting Christ for salvation and (2) if that fails, to keep people from living a victorious Christian life. He is diligent in pursuing those goals. His weapons are deception and untruths. He makes good use of his "devices" (2 Corinthians 2:11), "trickery and cunning craftiness" (Ephesians 4:14), and "wiles" or "schemes" (Ephesians 6:11, margin).

One of his most convincing tricks revolves around illicit sex. He cloaks the consequences, selling the pleasures and "benefits" of following his plan rather than God's. He "disguises himself as an angel of light" (2 Corinthians 11:14) and as a "friend" only trying to help us out of our frustration. He allures with bait designed to hook us. Since his promises of joy and fulfillment are built on lies, let us examine a few of those falsehoods the enemy attempts to sell us, myths and lies that form the appeal and drawing power of illicit sex in its variegated forms.

How the Process Works

The archdeceiver, Satan, uses mental tricks and circular reasoning to bring us to bizarre conclusions, like: Elephants are ugly. You are ugly. Therefore you are an elephant. This form of thinking begins with a truth but ends with a false conclusion. For example, one man who wanted to justify separating from his wife expressed: (1) God wants us to be happy, not miserable (a truth). (2) When my wife and I are together, we are miserable (this also may be true). (3) Conclusion: God does not want us to be together (untrue, a false conclusion). We must guard our hearts from this erroneous pattern of reasoning, for it gives Satan fertile soil to sow thoughts leading to distorted beliefs, imprudent decisions, and immoral behavior. A classic example of this gnarled, corkscrew thinking is the leader who fell in love with another woman and left his wife. He said, "God wants us to be happy. I'm not happy with my wife. I'm very happy with this woman. I'd rather go to hell with her than to heaven with my wife!"

Examples of Lies and Myths We Believe

- **"Sexual pleasure is better in an affair."** One of the myths that the beguiled man swallows is that sex with "the other woman" will be superior to that experienced in his marriage. Dr. Frank Pittman, mentioned earlier, affirms that although it is supposed that affairs revolve around spectacular sexual experiences, the reality is that many fallen husbands admit the sex was better at home.[38]

    Christian leader and author Tim Lahaye comments that after being accosted by a woman who offered herself to him, it really wasn't a serious temptation for him. The reason: he says a man happily married would never trade a Mercedes Benz in the garage for a VW Beetle Bug in the street.[39]

> *A happily married man would never trade a Mercedes Benz in the garage for a VW Beetle Bug in the street.*

- **"The affair will help."** Another myth is "an affair will help our marriage and solve our problems." The thinking goes like this: "I simply need a change of atmosphere, and then I'll return to my marriage with my mind cleared and

---

[38] Dr. Frank Pittman, *Private Lies*. Cited in the book, *Sex, a Man's Guide* by Stefan Bechtel y Laurence Roy Stains, Emmaus (Pennsylvania: Rodale Press, Inc.), 429.
[39] Tim Lahaye, *The Act of Marriage After 40* (Grand Rapids, Michigan: Zondervan Publishing House), 163.

without the stress and emotional anguish I suffered before. And with the affair, my sexual needs will be met and that will avoid a divorce, which will benefit our children." This is simply another instance of the myths with which the enemy charms and beguiles the undiscerning. The truth is that an affair only worsens our problems and situation while resolving nothing. Trying to escape a gale, we create a hurricane. Avoiding an affair will help the marriage, not taking a detour into one.

- **"I have everything under control."** Many believe they have it all coldly calculated and that they can quit the addiction or halt the affair whenever they choose. They forget that it becomes slavery, with emotions that often are embroiled, entangled, and enchained. Soul ties have been formed. And even if one is willing—and able—to call it off, the other person may not be. In some cases there are threats, accusations, or even blackmail, with large sums of hush money paid, if the relationship is aborted. Potiphar's wife, who seemed passionately in love with Joseph, became his enemy when he did not succumb to her enticements and in vengeance had him imprisoned (Genesis 39).

A story is told of a beautiful and powerful eagle that perched on a large block of ice floating just above Niagara Falls. Other birds warned him to flee the danger, but he retorted, "I am powerful, and with my strong wings I can lift off whenever I choose." When only a few feet from the falls, he lifted his majestic wings to fly, only to discover his claws were frozen to the ice.

Rather than trusting in our power of control, a better solution is to submit control of our lives (thoughts, attitudes, behavior) to the Holy Spirit. Only under His control do we really have control. To "walk in the Spirit" (Galatians 5:16–24) is to seek His wisdom and allow Him to be in the driver's seat. "God is my copilot" will not work. He is no one's copilot! He is pilot or He is not aboard. He is

Lord of all or He is not Lord at all. He alone has and shares the power to turn away from the slavery of illicit sex. Don't trust in the strength of your "wings" or your ability to beat the odds. Don't get "frozen to the ice."

- **"My sin will not hurt anyone."** A falsehood often believed is that our sin will have no deleterious effects on others. We've seen in earlier chapters examples of the devastating damage our sexual sin can produce. He who thinks otherwise is deceiving himself. It is a convenient pretext for one who well knows it doesn't square with the truth.

> *A falsehood we frequently believe is that our sin won't hurt anyone.*

Who gets hurt? Our spouse, our children, our parents, our coworkers, people under our leadership, unbelievers, even God. We've seen how our disobedience can wound His great heart of love. We not only hurt these persons, we *sin* against them. And of course we hurt ourselves and sin against our own body: "He who commits sexual immorality sins against his own body" (1 Corinthians 6:18).

- **"No one will know. My affair won't be discovered."** As we saw in chapter 1, the Word of God assures us: "Be sure your sin will find you out" (Numbers 32:23), and "whatever a man sows, that he will also reap" (Galatians 6:8). The illusion that "nobody will know" will turn to disillusion when our secret is discovered.

Almost everyone involved in an affair believes this myth. A pastor friend of mine and his lover concealed their illicit romance very well until the day someone saw them kissing between shelves in the public library of their city. King David believed he had gotten away with his baneful, lustful deeds, that God had forgotten about it by now (a whole year had passed), and that consequences were no longer an issue. But God sent Nathan the prophet to bring repentance and correction to David's life (2 Samuel 12). Another leader I know hid his sin for more than seven years, but one day his cell phone exposed the truth. However it happens, it is only a question of time until it does. "He who covers his sins will not prosper, but whoever confesses and forsakes them will have mercy" (Proverbs 28:13). And here's the clincher: "And there is no creature hidden from His sight, but all things *are* naked and open to the eyes of Him to whom we *must give* account" (Hebrews 4:13).

- **"God is blessing my ministry. There's much fruit. This is evidence that God approves what I'm doing."** The truth is that God blesses His people—even through a flawed ministry—because He loves them, not because He approves of sinful conduct in His leaders. The person who believes this is believing a lie. God, in His love and mercy, sends blessing even when his servants are living less-than-obedient lives. But we are never to take His blessing on our ministry as His approval of our life.
- **"God is a God of love, and if there is punishment for my conduct, it won't be a big deal. He understands my situation, and His grace will cover me."** Believing this refuse is as senseless and the man who prayed, "Lord, forgive me for the sin I'm about to commit." Jude 1:4 speaks of "ungodly men, who turn the grace of our God into licentiousness."

> *We are never to take His blessing on our ministry as His approval of our life.*

This means we issue ourselves a license to sin. The attitude says: "I can sin and suffer no consequences because God is a God of love and His grace guarantees me forgiveness." He *is* love and grace and mercy, but He is also a God of righteousness who chastens His disobedient children

(see Hebrews 12:5–6). His grace is not a license to sin but a power to not sin!
- **"Moral purity is impossible."** Some struggle with sexual impurity for a time, fail repeatedly, and finally give up. They believe moral purity is an impossible goal, that no one can actually live like that, so it's useless to keep trying. This is a self-evident falsehood because God wouldn't command something that is impossible. He has promised to give us power to resist the tempter, and no temptation or test is beyond the reach of His mighty ability.

> *His grace is not a license to sin but a power to not sin!*

Here's the promise:

> No temptation has overtaken you except such as is common to man; but God *is* faithful, who will not allow you to be tempted beyond what you are able, but with the temptation will also make the way of escape, that you may be able to bear *it*. (1 Corinthians 10:13)

We are holy only in His holiness, pure in His purity, wise in His wisdom, worthy in His worthiness, and strong in His strength. "Finally, my brethren, be strong in the Lord and in the power of His might" (Ephesians 6:10). The lie is: We can't. The truth is this: We can, in Him.
- **"If you were a better Christian, you wouldn't be tempted by sexual sin."** This myth pulls a dark cloud of depression and guilt over us for failing in the moral arena of life. As human beings, especially as men, sexual temptation is nothing abnormal. Temptation is a universal experience that comes to everyone. Jesus was "in all points tempted as

we are, yet without sin" (Hebrews 4:15). Temptation is not a sin, yielding to it *is*. How we respond to the seduction determines if we will live in victory or defeat.

- **"I married the wrong person."** In the midst of difficulties, pressures, and conflicts, or when we are bored with our marriage, it's easy to believe this whopper. It's another attempt to justify actions and decisions that cloak selfish desire and eventually prove disastrous.

The Bible speaks of the spirit of truth (the Holy Spirit, John 15:26) and the spirit of error (1 John 4:6), the latter being equivalent to the "deceiving spirits" mentioned by Paul in 1 Timothy 4:1. Following and obeying the Spirit of truth leads to a life of moral purity. Following and obeying the spirit of error leads to a life of lust and fallenness.

We cannot be guided by both simultaneously. If the destiny you desire is a life of freedom and purity that pleases and glorifies God, you must choose and follow the road that leads you there. The spirit of error conduces deeper into sexual enslavement. The Spirit of truth leads to liberation from that bondage. Rejecting the lie and embracing the truth will escort you to moral purity and sexual integrity. The adage is true: *If you don't change the direction you're going, you're liable to end up where you were headed.* "Sanctify them by Your truth, Your Word is truth." (John 17:17)

For Reflection

1. Have you ever believed any of the lies mentioned above? Which one?
2. What do you think of the assertion "an affair will help our marriage"?
3. Do you agree that our sin, if handled wisely, will bring no harm to anyone? Why do you believe as you do?
4. What steps can you take to reject the lies and follow the truth?

9

What Every Wife Should Know
Recipe for a Happy Husband

An excellent wife is the crown of her husband.
—Proverbs 12:4

*Houses and riches are an inheritance from fathers,
but a prudent wife is from the Lord.*
—Proverbs 19:14

Who can find a virtuous wife? For her worth is far above rubies.
—Proverbs 31:10

DANGEROUS CURVES

A wife plays a key role in the life of her husband as a defense against illicit sex. She, more than anyone else, can help her mate avoid the disgrace of a moral fall. God has placed in her heart and mind the intelligence and in her hands the power to change the course of a tempted, straying, "prone to wander" spouse. Or better yet, help avoid his wandering in the first place. People speak of the "guilty party" and the innocent one when there is infidelity. But even though the "innocent party" has not sinned, in many cases, she has consciously or unconsciously contributed to situations that become influences and affect decisions and actions of her spouse.

Often the decision of a tempted man to step over the line is a reaction to situations being experienced in the marriage. An affair can be birthed from the state of affairs at home. A prudent wife can be of incalculable value to her husband, detecting and preventing situations that can damage the relationship and nudge the husband over the edge.

> *A prudent wife can be of incalculable value to her husband.*

This is in no way an attempt to justify sinful actions of the husband, or to blame the wife. Rather, it is to identify and correct influences that call forth harmful effects in the relationship and exacerbate an already bad situation. In this chapter, the focus is on what the wife can do to defuse landmines before they detonate. The goal is protection of the marriage and motivation for the husband who needs to escape the seductive lure of illicit sex, whatever its form.

It has been estimated by experts in the field that at least 20 percent of believers' homes have been affected in some measure by infidelity. Consequently some practical and biblical counsel for wives with spouses prone to stray can be helpful. And if no problem is manifesting now, it can serve as preventive medicine to set up a line of defense and protect them from the often-devastating effects of illicit sex in the future.

WHAT EVERY WIFE SHOULD KNOW

Counsel for the Wife

Be willing to change. We all come to our marriages having been molded by ideas, attitudes, and customs learned in our respective families. Those ideas and attitudes were part of our formation because every home has its culture. The problem is that much of what we learned was not correct or healthy but errors committed by our parents. Our ideas about sexual intimacy in marriage, discipline of children, handling of finances, resolution of conflicts, etc., come from a less-than-perfect source but nonetheless may be all we know about these matters. The director of a family counseling service discovered that 80 percent of counselees were repeating the errors of their parents.

A husband's dissatisfaction with the intimate area of marriage may emanate from a wife's having learned from her mother that sex is a bothersome, annoying necessity. If this attitude is repeated in the wife, her spouse may back off from sex, feeling it is a burden to her. A caring man wants his wife to enjoy sex, not endure it. Tolerating it reduces the joy and satisfaction for him. A wise wife will be willing to change this or other taboo-type thinking in order to please her husband and increase sexual satisfaction for both. She will come to recognize that sex in marriage is a gift of God for the enjoyment, ecstasy, and delight of the couple. Flexibility and willingness to change enhances the relationship, a balm that brings healing to this and other areas of their marriage. On the other hand, intransigence produces stagnation, frustration, and potential temptation to find what he is not finding in his marriage.

Don't be naïve. Why are so many wives devastated upon learning of their spouses' infidelity? Because they thought, "That could never happen in our marriage!" There's a fine line between trust in a spouse (healthy) and naiveté (unhealthy). Having confidence in the spouse is noble, failing to exercise caution and discernment is not.

> *Having confidence in the spouse is noble, failing to exercise caution and discernment is not.*

On the other hand, a wife should not be unreasonably jealous, suspecting every move of her spouse, imagining things that aren't happening and breeding mistrust that can damage the relationship. Finding a balance between the two extremes is not easy. The wisest route is to trust the spouse (if there are no viable reasons for doubt). In any case, discernment and alertness are always in vogue. Please remember something I said in the beginning of the book: No one is exempt from the possibility of temptation in this area—absolutely no one! Remembering this can help us take the necessary steps to build a marriage that is "affair-proof."

Know the needs of your spouse and try to meet them.

- *The masculine need for sexual expression.*

One day the wife of a friend of ours said something humorous and at the same time a great truth: "I feed my dog well so he won't have to eat garbage in the streets and refuse dumps." Of course, she meant she supplied his sexual needs to avoid his getting them met by the sexual "garbage" of unfaithfulness. She was a wise woman because, instead of being ingenuous and thinking, "My husband would never consider such a thing," she recognized he was made of flesh and blood, with desires and sexual needs that should be met. The same is true in the case of a wife. Paul speaks of both in this passage from the Message Bible:

> Sexual drives are strong, but marriage is strong enough to contain them and provide for a balanced and fulfilling sexual life in a world of sexual disorder. The marriage bed must be a place of mutuality—the husband seeking to satisfy his wife, the wife seeking to satisfy her husband. Marriage is not a place to "stand up for your rights." Marriage is a decision to serve the other, whether in bed or out. Abstaining from

sex is permissible for a period of time if you both agree to it, and if it's for the purposes of prayer and fasting—but only for such times. Then come back together again. Satan has an ingenious way of tempting us when we least expect it. (1 Corinthians 7:3–5)

The core idea in this scriptural command is the obligation of each to satisfy the sexual needs of the other to eliminate the temptation of infidelity. Mutuality is the name of the game. "Do not deprive one another" (ver. 5). Needless to say, many men are negligent in meeting the emotional and love needs of their wives. However, in this chapter, we're discussing how the wife can help her husband by meeting *his* needs. A paraphrase of verse five could be: "Wives, do not deprive your husband of sexual satisfaction. Meet his needs." Verse 2 says, "But because of sexual immorality, [temptation] let each man have his own wife" (author's emphasis). Translation: a man whose sexual needs are not met is vulnerable to sexual temptation. "Let each man have his own wife" in this context means that she is the one to satisfy his need for sexual expression.

The prudent wife will recognize that her husband, if he is a normal man, has an almost insatiable appetite for sexual intimacy. The wife must "feed" him well, remembering that a hungry man looks for food, and if he doesn't find it at home, he will be tempted to eat elsewhere. Someone has wisely said, "If you don't satisfy the needs of your mate, others are awaiting the opportunity to do so." Unfortunately, this is true.

> *The prudent wife will recognize that her husband, if he is a normal man, has an almost insatiable appetite for sexual intimacy.*

Prudent wives remember that a man is sexually very different from a woman. The *Creator* designed and wired him with a different voltage. Many wives do not understand why their husband needs sexual expression so often. The man usually has great energy for sex. The reason? According to Dr. James Dobson, a Christian psychologist, the male body has, beside the prostate, two tiny pouches that contain semen. When they are vacated during sex, they require some seventy-two hours—three days—to refill. When this happens, a man will again become susceptible to sexual stimuli as the sexual energy begins to build anew. A healthy man can typically need sex every three or four days. The average frequency of sex in the United States is 2.6 times per week.

Lack of understanding of these male characteristics can mar the relationship in marriage and throw a pail of cold water on the intimate life of the couple. Some women believe they married a "pervert" when they discover how much sex their husbands desire. Many then realize it's a masculine need they were unaware of. One woman complained to her counselor, "I don't know why my husband needs sex so often. If I permitted it, he would want sex every month!" Another wife expressed, "I failed to recognize how intense are the temptations for a man and how much strength is needed to not exceed the limits established by God."

A Christian wife said, "It was surprising to me to learn how different men are from women. It astonished me that Christian men can have that problem [of sexual temptation] even after marrying." Another commentary: "The attraction I felt as a single woman upon seeing a man was nothing compared to that which a man feels when seeing a woman." Another woman commented, "Because we women don't have that problem, it seems to us that some men are perverts who are out of control and only think about sex."

> *A wife should remember that a man is sexually very different from a woman.*

The amazement that some women feel—that a husband can have these kinds of battles—is a barrier to open communication about sexual problems in marriage. When a wife was asked how she would feel if she knew her husband battled temptations, she replied, "I would kill him!" This attitude closes the door to a husband who may like to talk with his wife about his struggles. Another wife expressed, "I was surprised that married men can have so many problems in that area." And still another wife grieved, "When my husband and I broached the subject, I felt angry, wounded, and betrayed. I couldn't understand why he still looked at other women."

A posture of understanding and desiring to support and assist the husband creates a different atmosphere—one in which a husband can seek the help of his wife. A discerning wife expressed, "When I asked my husband, he was honest and confessed he had had struggles. At first I felt hurt, but then I gave thanks to God for his honesty." Another spouse commented, "I recognize my husband is bombarded daily with sexual images and innuendos. I want to know about his daily brushes with temptation in order to understand him better. I didn't feel betrayed because he has been faithful. Other women are not so fortunate."[40]

- ***The need for respect and admiration.*** One of the most important needs God built into a man is to be respected. The Word of God confirms this: "Let each one of you in particular so love his own wife as himself, and let the wife see that she respects her husband" (Ephesians 5:33). When a wife does not show respect, it carves a void in him, causing him to feel less a man. His sense of manhood erodes. On the other hand, the respect and admiration of his spouse fulfills him, leaving him with no need to "prove his masculinity." His manfulness must be affirmed and strengthened by his wife. When that need is not met, the emptiness lingers inside him. Sooner or later, a temptation will emerge in the form of a woman who will compensate for the admi-

---

[40] Some of the commentaries of this section were taken from the excellent book *Every Man's Battle* by Stephen Arterburn y Fred Stoeker, (Colorado Springs, Colorado: Waterbrook Press, 2000), 33–35.

ration and respect he doesn't receive at home. Wise is the spouse who realizes her husband's road is rife with dangerous curves, and helps him see and heed the signs in time.

- ***The need for companionship in her husband's "world."*** Oftentimes a man feels his wife has no interest in things that are important to him, including his work, a sport, a pastime such as fishing or hunting, some diversion outside the home, or even his ministry or leadership in the church. The participation, companionship, and presence of the wife in the world of her husband help to create closeness and strengthen the marriage. I've known cases where the wife refused to be a part of her husband's world, which contributed to the deterioration of the relationship. One wise wife, on the other hand, was weary of her husband's spending so much time at home with his pastime—a laboratory. Finally she made a decision. She went to the public library and read and studied books on chemicals, experiments, etc. When she had gained a fair amount of knowledge, she entered her husband's lab one evening and began talking to him about what interested him. He was astonished but pleased beyond words, which began a new closeness and companionship that enriched their marriage.

- ***Emotional needs.*** There are of course emotional needs in both partners, but at present, we're focusing on those of the husband. His self-esteem, his sense of value as a person and as a man, his need to love and be loved, the need for approval, to know he is the most important man in the world to his wife, and other emotional needs should be met primarily by his wife. Marriage is the most intimate of all human relationships and is the most obvious and ideal context for these needs to be met. When that happens, the husband feels happy and fulfilled. When it doesn't, he feels frustrated. Such frustration has led many men to land in a ditch on a dangerous curve. Frustration from unmet needs is a sign that should be heeded by both partners.

WHAT EVERY WIFE SHOULD KNOW

The "Love Bank"

Every marriage has a love bank. Both partners have an account in it. When he meets a need in her life, a deposit is made in his account. When he only takes and doesn't give (love, attention, caresses, serving, respect, consideration, etc.), he makes a withdrawal from his account. The same of course is true of her and her account in the love bank. As in a regular bank account, if only withdrawals and no deposits are made, the account is soon overdrawn. Checks begin to bounce as our funds are depleted. In marriage, as our "balance" descends to zero, we lose our capacity to love due to a lack of "funds," and the marriage is in trouble.

> *We feel attraction toward a person who deposits in our emotional love bank.*

At this stage, someone outside the marriage may open a new account and deposit in it, meeting unmet needs in the life of the husband or wife. When the wife, for example, has not made deposits (met needs in her husband's life) and another woman is making big deposits, a dangerous curve is being approached. We feel attraction toward a person who deposits in our emotional love bank.

I am aware that many husbands need to learn to treat their wives with tenderness and consideration, change habits and customs that irritate and hurt their spouse, and give their wives the love they need through words of appreciation, acts of kindness, and nonsexual caresses.

> *For a man, sex is the key that expands his capacity to love.*

Many men need to learn to deposit in their wife's emotional bank. A man needs to learn that for a woman, love comes before sex and is the key that opens her to enjoy sexual intimacy. And the woman needs to know that for a man, sex is the key that kindles and expands his capacity to love.

I am convinced that if wives try to understand their husbands, please them sexually, open up to converse with them about sex, and deposit generously in their love bank account, much will change, and they will see an evident improvement in all the areas of their marriage.

For Reflection

1. Why is the wife an important key as a defense against sexual sin for her husband?
2. How can a woman strengthen her marriage through knowing and meeting the masculine needs of her husband?
3. How can a woman deposit more in her account in the marriage love bank?
4. Do you believe it's true that many women don't fully understand the sexual needs of men?
5. How can a woman overcome her lack of understanding in this area in order to strengthen physical intimacy in her marriage and increase her husband's level of sexual satisfaction?

10

In Search of Moral Purity
Navigating the Dangerous Curves

*He will redeem my soul from going down to the Pit,
And my life shall see the light.*
—Job 33:28 (NKJV, marginal reading)

Some of those reading this book are now caught in a trap of illicit sex. Others may be treading on the icy edge of a precipice, eyeing the forbidden fruit. Applying a biblical phrase, they are taking "fire to [their] bosom" and walking "on hot coals." Whatever the case, I believe the counsel of this and the following chapter will help to free those fighting a sexual battle to escape from the dark pit. There is help for those who have fallen and for those on a slippery slope, those with a propensity to take the bait of moral temptation. God desires that all His children live in truth and freedom. His will is that we "be strong in the Lord and in the power of His might, and that we can "stand against the wiles [margin: *schemings*] of the devil" (Ephesians 6:10–11).

Free from the Trap

In frontier days, many "wolfers" and other trappers set snares for animals in order to sell the furs. An animal with its leg caught in a trap was a pathetic sight as it struggled to free itself from the snare. Often it was willing to break or tear its leg off to get free. A more pathetic sight is a man beguiled and ensnared by temptation's allurement. What he thought would be a feast of pleasure turned out to be a mockery, or what someone described as "honeyed poison."

This is a true picture of persons caught in the trap of illicit sex. They cannot escape whenever they desire or in their own strength but when they trust God to free them from their entrapment. Jesus is the *Liberator* who sets us free. Or to use another metaphor, He's the one who pulls us out of the quicksand.

To some, freedom may seem elusive and even impossible. It's true that sexual sin and its enticement are strong and can be almost impossible to conquer in our own strength. Jesus exhorted us: "Watch and pray, lest you enter into temptation. The spirit indeed is willing, but the flesh is weak" (Matthew 26:41). Once the trap springs, the enemy does not easily release his prey. However, many who were once enslaved by illicit sex are now free and even helping others to gain freedom.

Christ longs to rescue, restore, and redeem from the pit. As the psalmist David discovered, "I waited patiently for the Lord; and He inclined to me and heard my cry. He also brought me up out of a horrible pit, out of the miry clay, and set my feet upon a rock, *and established my steps*" (Psalm 40:1–2). His blood cleanses us from sin when there is true repentance. Freedom is possible if we are willing to pay the price. God has placed a ladder in the pit for us to escape, if we will but take the necessary steps.

Steps Toward Freedom

A Passion to be Free. The first step in leaving the abyss, whether of adultery, fornication, pornography, homosexuality, lascivia, or other form of illicit sex, is desiring freedom with a passion. The avidity to leave the pit must outweigh the desire for the pleasures and "benefits" received from the practice of those activities. We must crave a life of transformation and purity. When the carnal desires attract us more than purity, it's not possible to climb out of the hole.

> *When carnal desires attract us more than purity, it's not possible to climb out of the hole.*

Moses had to choose between the wealth and power of Egypt (symbol of the world) and obedience to God. He "refused to be called the son of Pharaoh's daughter, choosing rather to suffer affliction with the people of God than to enjoy the passing pleasures of sin, esteeming the reproach of Christ greater riches than the treasures in Egypt; for he looked to the reward" (Hebrews 11:24–26). Like Moses, we must all evaluate and choose: Which has greater value, the transitory pleasures of our sin or the *reward*, which is freedom, God's smile, and a life of victory and moral purity?

Part of the reward is the ability to finish our course, having lived a life pleasing to God, and had a ministry that's fruitful and useful to Him and others. Paul told Timothy, "Fulfill your ministry" (2 Timothy 4:5b), and to the Colossians, he wrote, "And say to Archippus, 'Take heed to the ministry which you have received in the Lord, that you may fulfill it'" (4:17). The reward of finishing our course with God's approval has no equal. What Paul desired for Timothy and Archippus, he craved for himself as well: "But none of these things move me; nor do I count my life dear to myself, so that I may finish my race with joy, and the ministry which I received from the Lord Jesus" (Acts 20:24).

I have dealt with believers and leaders who rejected the process of restoration—some due to pride, love for their sin, lack of true repentance, or simply reluctance to face problematic issues in their lives. Some are out of the ministry or leadership today; others continue in an "illegitimate ministry," having rejected restoration. But those who go the distance and embrace redemption, recover, rebuild, and reestablish a fruitful ministry and a life of moral purity and sexual integrity.

Greed and lust are iniquitous desires very opposite of love for purity. When a man or woman renounces—once and for all—the lust that dominated them and develops a passion for liberty in Christ, they have taken the first step toward freeing themselves from the bondage of sexual sin. To be free, we have to crave freedom with all our heart.

> *To be free, we have to crave freedom with all our heart.*

A Passion for God. It's not sufficient to have a strong desire to be free; we must also possess a zeal for God. We cannot remove darkness from a room by any means other than turning on a light. When the light comes on, the darkness cringes and flees. How can we turn on God's light? Jesus is light. The Word of God is light. Falling in love with Christ and His Word flood our souls with spiritual illumination that enables us to walk in victory, free from the darkness and seduction of illicit sex. Ignorance gives way to knowledge, and carelessness to a heightened awareness and diligence. Here's a directive from the Bible that turns on the light of our understanding:

> For you were once darkness, but now *you are* light in the Lord. Walk as children of light (for the fruit of the Spirit *is* in all goodness, righteousness, and truth), finding out what is acceptable to the Lord. And have no fellowship with the unfruitful works of darkness, but rather expose *them*. For it is shameful even to speak of those things which are done by them in secret. But all things that are exposed are made manifest by the light, for whatever makes manifest is light. Therefore He says: "Awake, you who sleep, arise from the dead, and Christ will give you light." (Ephesians 5:8–14)

When our passion for God outweighs our lust for sexual pleasure, our life will fill with light. And that light will expel the darkness, for darkness and light cannot occupy the same space at the same time.

Hatred for Sin. A man who was battling sexual sin commented to his pastor: "I'm still doing it. I suppose I still don't hate it enough to stop." A fascinating verse in Psalms 45:7 prophesies of Jesus: "You love righteousness and hate wickedness; therefore God, Your God, has anointed You with the oil of gladness more than Your companions." Hating sin and loving righteousness is a prerequisite for gaining and maintaining victory over sexual bondage. I heard a humorous story about some believers who were trying, unsuccessfully, to cast a demon of lust out of a man. When asked why he thought it wasn't working, the man replied, "Because I like it!" A classic example of "men loved darkness rather than light, because their deeds were evil" (John 3:19b).

God is a holy God, and as such, sin is abhorrent to Him. Many sins in the Bible are labeled as "abominations to God." An abomination is something extremely repugnant and repulsive. "God is light and in Him is no darkness at all." This is why He wants His children to be free of the entanglements and crippling effects of sin. He desires that we adopt the same attitude toward sin that He holds. One of the meanings of repentance is altering our thinking about sin until it aligns with His. Our daily prayer should be: "Lord, give me a clean mind and a pure heart. Grant me a love for righteousness and purity and a hatred for sin."

> I hate every false way. (Psalm 119:104)
> The fear of the Lord is to hate evil. (Proverbs 8:13)
> Hate evil, love good. (Amos 5:15)
> Abhor what is evil. Cling to what is good. (Romans 12:9)
> And this you have, that you hate the deeds of the Nicolaitans, which I also hate. (Revelation 2:6)

Honesty. Being honest with God, with others, and with one's self is another vital principle for navigating the dangerous curves. Part of the armor of God is "having girded your waist with truth" (Ephesians 6:14). The apostle John told his readers, "I have no greater joy than to hear that my children walk in truth" (3 John, v. 4). These words also reflect the heart of our heavenly Father for His children today.

> *When one is trapped in sexual aberrations, in many cases there is a double life, secrets, cover-up, and lies.*

The Greek word for "truth" means that which is true and free from deception, falsehood, simulation, hypocrisy, or lies. It speaks of authenticity and transparency in one's life. When one is trapped in sexual aberrations, in many cases there is a double life, secrets, cover-up, and lies. "Therefore, putting away lying, each one speak truth with his neighbor" (Ephesians 4:25). Becoming truthful and accountable requires the following:

- **Acknowledgement of Sin.** It is crucial to recognize our sexual practices that are outside God's plan as sin. They are not simply mistakes, weaknesses, flubs, foul-ups, indiscretions, blunders, boners, boo-boos, failures, misdeeds, slipups, glitches, miscues, or goofs. They are sins committed against God and others. They break God's moral law. They are nails in the hands and feet of Jesus. We must not only acknowledge our sins as such but also the hurt they have inflicted on others.

- **True Repentance.** Repentance is not restoration, but it opens the door to it and enables the process to begin. Many believe their repentance equals restoration. That only clears the ground of rubble so that rebuilding can commence. Repentance is a profound change of attitude about God, sin, and ourselves. We no longer see God as a divine killjoy, squelching our fun. Sin is now seen as an ugly force, separating us from God's best. We cease seeing ourselves as victims or people who have some deserved perks and entitlements coming. Genuine repentance is indispensable for genuine restoration. The fruit of repentance is not only changed minds but transformed conduct. John the Baptist told his listeners, "Therefore bear fruits worthy of repentance" (Matthew 3:8). The Amplified Bible says it best: "So produce fruit that is consistent with repentance [demonstrating new behavior that proves a change of heart, and a conscious decision to turn away from sin]." True repentance is turning our back on our sin and embracing a life of moral purity.

Stop Blaming Others. This is another way of camouflaging and justifying our waywardness. The blame game is as old as Eden and as futile. Other people or factors played a role in our fall, but we are the ones who said *yes* and gave temptation a green light.

> *True repentance is turning our back on our sin and embracing a life of moral purity.*

A woman who left her husband to marry another man said she prayed that if her action wasn't God's will, He would remove the desire she felt for him. When that didn't happen, she concluded God was approving her decision and proceeded with her plan, destroying her marriage and wrecking her family. God has given us His Word to guide our moral decisions, not subjective feelings and phony prayers. To progress in true change and restoration, we must assume the responsibility and accept the consequences of our actions and cease blaming others. I recently read a story about an old sea captain who constantly got lost at sea. A number of rescues were mobilized by his friends, who finally gave him a compass. The next time out, he again became lost and, exasperated, even threw the compass away. When his friends asked why, he responded, "Because every time I wanted to go a certain direction, the compass pointed in another." The Bible points us in the right direction. We get lost when we discard it and go our own way.

Recognize the Source of Moral Purity. We do not, in ourselves, possess holiness. On the contrary, if we give free rein to our heart, there is a law of spiritual "gravity" that pulls us down into the perverse and sinful. Jeremiah 17:9 reminds us, "The heart is deceitful above all things, and desperately wicked; who can know it?" True godliness comes only from God when He deposits it in us by the Holy Spirit. In other words, as stated earlier, we are only holy in His imputed holiness. Moral purity isn't something we can produce. It's something God deposits in our account when we believe for it and then walk it out.

Get Unstuck from the Muck. Total separation from persons, places, objects, and influences that can present temptation is essential. If we have maintained an improper relationship with a person or frequented certain places or used certain objects (porno videos and magazines, Internet, etc.), disengagement and dissociation from those things is imperative. It's impossible to win the victory and crawl out of the abyss with one foot still stuck in the muck.

Old associations not severed and abandoned can create a propensity to return to old ways. A leader caught in the web of pornography was discovered and in time restored. After a time, he returned to ministry. Before his fall, he had used porno DVDs, and instead of destroying them at the time of restoration, he *stored* them! Six months after returning to a ministry position, in a moment of weakness and temptation, he dug out the hidden DVDs. Not unlinking from the old "stuff" is an invitation to a relapse.

Acceptance of Help from Others. To truly and fully escape from the illicit sex trap, receiving help from others is vital. The power of temptation and the tendency to relapse complicates getting free from the pit and retards restoration. The caring heart and extended arm of a friend are of inestimable help in getting out of the "horrible pit" and the "miry clay."

> *Few people have the power to climb out of the pit without the help of others.*

There's no room here for self-sufficiency and bravado. Humility accepts help; pride rejects it and is a recipe for disaster. Also available is help from pastors, counselors, and other mature leaders who dedicate to assisting fellow pilgrims on the road to recovery. Many of these are trained and capable of leading a process of restoration. Few people have the power to climb out of the pit without the help of others. And of course, the love and power of God are available to the person who is truly repentant and seeks Him with a sincere heart (see Isaiah 41:10; 1 Corinthians 10:13; Hebrews 2:18, 4:15–16; 2 Peter 2:9).

Be Patient. Restoration and freedom are a process, not a magic wand, or a matter of a single prayer or counseling session. They are the outgrowth of learning new habits, renewing the mind, clinging to God's Word, and forming new life patterns. An obedient heart must be cultivated and nourished. Some fallen leaders I've worked with wanted to bypass the process and return almost immediately to leadership or ministry. This short-circuits the Spirit's work, impedes the progress, and can even abort restoration. Patience allows necessary factors to work toward the goal of recovery and rebuilding. Impatience interrupts and wreaks havoc on the process.

Drawing Near to God. It is an essential part of maintaining victory. The natural thing in these scenarios is to distance ourselves from Him, either from a cold heart or from a sense of shame or fear. And so we neglect our fellowship with Him, which only entangles and delays the solution. In doing so, we close ourselves off from our source of rescue. Remember, God still loves you. His disapproval of your behavior does not repeal His love for you. He loves you with an eternal love: "Yes, I have loved you with an everlasting love; therefore with lovingkindness I have drawn you" (Jeremiah 31:3). Your destination is not disaster; your destiny is restoration and renewal. There is hope; follow these steps, and they will lead you to victory.

11

How to Resist Temptation and Finish Well
Finding the Boundaries that Protect

One of the first sayings I learned in Spanish was: *It's better to prevent than to lament.* Sounds like: "An ounce of prevention is worth a pound of cure." Many are in trouble in their moral life due to desires, thoughts, feelings, habits, propensities, and behavior, which, if not corrected are a recipe for disaster. How then can we put that ounce of prevention to work, keeping us from fellowshipping with "the unfruitful works of darkness" (Ephesians 5:11) and cultivating moral purity?

DANGEROUS CURVES

Guardrails

Earlier I described some of the warning signs placed on roadways to alert us to danger. Such signs are vital, and the wise heed them. At times, in addition to signs, we need a guardrail to keep us out of a ravine. Signs warn us; guardrails protect us.

Rufino, a good friend of mine, was traveling in a bus with several family members and friends. Just above the city of Matagalpa in a mountainous region of central Nicaragua, the brakes failed as the bus rounded a dangerous curve and plunged downward into a canyon at full speed. Rufino's daughter-in-law was killed, and his son, Carlos, suffered a broken leg and other injuries. A pastor and his wife and son, friends of Rufino's, were killed, plus other deaths and injuries.

> *If a guardrail of sufficient strength had been placed on that curve, probably the accident would have been avoided and several lives saved.*

It was a double tragedy because they were returning from the funeral service of Rufino's wife, who had died a few days earlier of cancer. If a guardrail of sufficient strength had been placed on that curve, probably the accident would have been avoided and several lives saved. The lesson: when our brakes fail, we need a guardrail! I think of our "brakes" as the inner power to say no to temptation, and the "guardrail" as something outside ourselves that intervenes to save us from a moral catastrophe. That "something" must be established beforehand as boundaries, or "security measures."

What are some boundaries that can help us avoid a fall and gain victory over illicit sex of whatever ilk? They are restraints we can establish whether or not we are presently battling sexual temptation. Preventive medicine is always preferable to the curative kind. To stay out of the pit is easier than struggling to climb out.

HOW TO RESIST TEMPTATION AND FINISH WELL

> *Signs warn us; guardrails protect us.*

The problem is so epidemic and universal that probably a day doesn't pass without a number of believers and leaders somewhere on the planet sliding into that abyss. Not one, but many. For every one that falls, many more are on the slippery edge, drawn by temptation's enticement, listening to its promises, and flirting with its pleasures. Determine today you will not be another statistic.

Final Considerations

1. **Take an honest inventory of your life and current situation.** If you discover any improper thoughts, feelings, attitudes, or conduct, determine to address them with brutal honesty. This means shedding wrong impulses, tendencies, and habits as a snake sheds its old skin. You have to call it what it is in fact: iniquity and sin. You must reject all attempts to justify it, and then renounce it in the name of Jesus. Adopt the attitude of the psalmist, who prayed: "Search me, O God, and know my heart; try me, and know my anxieties; And see if *there is any* wicked way in me, and lead me in the way everlasting" (Psalms 139:23–24, NKJV).

    Some searching questions. Our inventory must be sincere (unfeigned) and according to truth. The psalmist also prayed: "Behold, You desire truth in the inward parts, and in the hidden part You will make me to know wisdom" (Psalms 51:6). Truth begets wisdom, and wisdom will keep us out of the snare. Are there any risk factors in any area of your life? What signs of precaution exist in your current situation? Is there a relationship you should break off? What habits or practices are you now permitting that you should renounce? And finally, what do you need to change to exit the risk zone?

2. **Make a pact with moral purity.**

The apostle Paul counsels us in 1 Corinthians 6:13, "Now the body is not for sexual immorality but for the Lord, and the Lord for the body." The only reason we have a physical body is to do the will of God in this life. Chapter 6 of Romans reminds us that the members of our physical body are not to be offered to sin "as instruments of iniquity," but rather "presented to God as instruments of righteousness" (v. 13). We are not to allow sin to reign in our bodies, because that leads to obeying lust (v. 12). Jesus taught us that, "whoever commits sin is a slave of sin" (John 8:34). Determine today that you will not be a slave of sexual aberrations.

> *The only reason we have a physical body is to do the will of God in this life.*

One way to establish that pact with moral purity is to make a covenant with our eyes, which are the doorway to our heart and mind. The eye gate is where temptation most often enters, peddling its wares. Seeing an attractive new car makes us desire it. When Eve *saw* the forbidden fruit, she took and then partook. She *saw* that it was "pleasant to the eyes and...desirable" (Genesis 3:6). On the other hand, Job declared, "I have made a covenant with my eyes; why then should I look upon a young woman [with lust]?" (author's emphasis, Job 31:1). The NIV translates it, "I made a covenant with my eyes not to look lustfully at a young woman."

Jesus said that when we look at a woman with lust, that is, with sexual desire, we have committed adultery with her in our heart. The apostle John, along with "the lust of the flesh" and "the pride of life," mentions "the lust of the eyes" as belonging to this world and something to which we should not become enslaved (see 1 John 2:15–17).

The way we look at a person of the opposite sex, the images we invite in, whether television, videos, magazines, Internet, or any other media, influence us and determine victory or defeat in our inner life.

3. **Change your thoughts and renew your mind.** The thoughts we allow in our minds are the root of either good or bad fruit in our lives. Our thoughts generate our feelings. Our feelings produce the decisions we make which in turn beget our actions, or conduct. Our actions then create the situations in which we live.

> Thoughts ▶ Feelings ▶ Decisions ▶ Actions ▶ Situations

The process, seen in reverse, means: if we desire different situations in our lives, we have to change our actions. To adjust them, we must learn to make wise decisions. To make prudent decisions we have to change the way we feel (since we normally decide based on feelings rather than reason). But to alter the way we feel about persons or things, we have to metamorphose our way of thinking. The Bible calls this renewing our mind.

So if we desire a different outcome, we have to change the way we think about victory in our moral life. Only a simpleton believes he can keep doing the same things and obtain a different result. If the new situations we desire are the respect of others, a clean conscience, a pure heart, a blessed marriage, an unsoiled testimony, and great relationships with others, then the shortest route to that destination is to renew our minds. Lustful thoughts produce lustful situations.

> *Only a simpleton believes he can keep doing the same things and obtain a different result.*

Pure thoughts create situations of moral purity and sexual integrity. Paul counseled Timothy, "Keep yourself pure" (1 Timothy 5:22), and purity begins in the mind. Someone has said that: Our predominant thoughts determine the direction of our life. God commands: "Be transformed by the renewing of your mind" (Romans 12:2). And in Ephesians 4:23, he commands: "Be renewed in the spirit of your mind." But how do we renew our minds?

Firstly, by saturating the mind with God's Word. When we align our thinking with His Word, our mind is filling with God's thoughts. His thoughts cleanse and transform ours. "You are already clean because of the word which I have spoken to you," said Jesus to His disciples (John 15:3). We can train our minds to think differently. Secondly, we remake our way of thinking by taking captive to Jesus every thought or feeling that is contrary to His will. "For the weapons of our warfare *are* not carnal but mighty in God for pulling down strongholds, casting down arguments and every high thing that exalts itself against the knowledge of God, bringing every thought into captivity to the obedience of Christ" (2 Corinthians 10:4–5). To fill our minds with the powerful principles of the Bible is to fill it with God's wisdom, thus creating guardrails of protection for our minds.

We are not to let ourselves be influenced by the world but to live in purity even amid the perversion and sexual provocation that surround us in our sexually charged societies. Morally, Corinth was called the "sewer" of Greece, and yet Paul exhorted the believers there to "flee sexual immorality" (1 Corinthians 6:18) and live in moral integrity. This begins with changing our thoughts about the following:

- ***God.*** He expects holiness in His people. "Be holy, for I am holy" (1 Peter 1:16).
- ***People.*** They are there, not to be used, but respected. A well-known minister confessed that in his youth and before knowing Christ, he considered girls to be "just a piece of meat" to be enjoyed.

- ***The Bible.*** We begin to love its words, even when it reproves us for wrong conduct. We seek its wisdom daily. We determine to obey its teachings.

  All Scripture *is* given by inspiration of God, and *is* profitable for doctrine, for reproof, for correction, for instruction in righteousness, that the man of God may be complete, thoroughly equipped for every good work. (2 Timothy 3:16–17)

- ***Sin.*** We no longer justify and make excuses for what the Bible reveals as wrong moral behavior. We ask forgiveness when appropriate and genuinely attempt to live in moral integrity. The Bible speaks of the "deceitfulness of sin" (Hebrews 3:13). We remind ourselves that sin is not a friend but an enemy set on deceiving and destroying us.

4. **Learn the power of discipline.** Self-discipline is doing what we should—not what we desire or feel like doing. Disciplined people are not controlled by their emotions and desires but guided by wise and healthy thoughts and decisions. Discipline is self-government. The disciplined person can wait for God's timing and His way of doing things and has learned to say *no* to wrong actions and *yes* to that which is right.

Disciplining our actions includes those of our physical body. Sexual purity demands discipline of the flesh. The apostle Paul asks: "Do you not know that your bodies are members of Christ? Shall I then take the members of Christ and make them members of a harlot?" He answers his own question: "Certainly not!" (1 Corinthians 6:15). This assures us that we have power over our bodies. "Do not let sin reign in your mortal body, that you should obey it in its lusts" (Romans 6:12). In effect, God is saying, "Don't obey your body.

Make your body obey you!" If such were not possible, God would not have given us these instructions. If we desire the blessing and approval of God in this area, we must exercise our sexual life as He has ordained and not in our own way.

God is not a heavenly killjoy, waiting to dampen the joy of our sexuality with rules, restrictions, and prohibitions. On the contrary, He who created our sexuality gave us one of the most beautiful gifts bestowed on humankind. His desire is that our sexuality be a fountain of blessing and happiness. Discipline in this area of life will win for us the prize of true joy, fulfillment, and pleasure.

> *Don't obey your body. Make your body obey you!*

Discipline of desire makes it possible to drink from a spring of clean, pure, and thirst-quenching sex that truly satisfies—not a mirage or a stagnant, polluted pool. A military general commented that the strength of Roman soldiers was not in their bravery but in their discipline. For us also this is the difference between victory and defeat in our moral life.

5. **Remember that you *can* resist temptation.** One of the favorite tricks of our enemy, Satan, is to make us believe that we are weak human beings, incapable of resisting sexual temptation (in whatever form). But God preempted the enemy with this promise from 1 Corinthians 10:13,

> No temptation has overtaken you except such as is common to man; but God *is* faithful, who will not allow you to be tempted beyond what you are able, but with the temptation will also make the way of escape, that you may be able to bear *it*.

Let's analyze this promise:

- No temptation we encounter is brand new, or something no one else has ever faced.
- God is faithful. We can totally count on His help. Jeremiah 33:3 says, "Call to me, and I will answer you, and show you great and mighty things which you do not know."
- He will not permit us to be tempted beyond our ability to resist and say no.
- He promised to give us a "way of escape" from the power of temptation. There is always a door—an exit—that we can take.
- So we never have the excuse that "the temptation was too strong to resist."

In every temptation we *can* be victorious. God has promised that we can be "more than conquerors" (Romans 8:37). It is possible to be triumphant in all sexual seduction or enticement. We can be winners, not losers and victims. To know that we *never* have to suffer defeat in our moral and sexual life is a giant step forward to living in victory.

6. **Careful with those out-of-town trips.** Travel is part and parcel of the work of many business executives, salespersons, leaders, and pastors; it can't be avoided. But we can take needed precautions to reduce the risk of a subtle and unexpected coaxing into a trap. How can we accomplish that?

   - *Always carry a photo of your spouse and family and place it where you will see it often.* It reminds us that people we love and don't want to hurt are waiting for us at home. Our children are counting on us to act with integrity, which will enable them to continue respecting us as dad, hero, and example.

- *Limit your absences.* Some trips are inevitable and can be of great blessing. But an excess of absences from home can be undermining to marriage and family life. Too much absenteeism can produce loneliness in the spouse and expose her to unnecessary temptation. Remember that nobody—absolutely nobody—is exempt from the possibility of being allured in this area. Many men have paid an appalling price for leaving their mates alone too much. And not only the mate, but the children are exposed to needless temptations. I have known cases in which the excessive absence of parents provided opportunities for their children to become involved in immorality, alcoholism, drugs, etc. In some cases, these were PKs (pastors' kids). Taking necessary precautions can save us—and our families—from unnecessary grief!
- *Don't travel alone (unless absolutely unavoidable).* We are more vulnerable to temptation when out of our normal environs. Factors that normally provide accountability are absent. Temptation has more pull, and our only "brakes" are ones we have built in. Whenever possible, travel with your spouse or a ministry colleague or friend. This practice is a precaution from unexpected dangerous curves along the way.

> **We are more vulnerable to temptation when we are out of our normal environs.**

- *Stay in contact with your family.* When traveling away from home, frequent contact by phone, e-mail, or social media is a good way to let your family know you care about them, though not physically present. This strengthens family ties and adds power to resist temptation. It's a shield of protection against the fiery darts of the enemy. Hearing our mate's voice helps stifle the voice of the tempter.

"For me, success is returning home after a business or ministry trip with a clean conscience and the joy of knowing I have been faithful to my God and my family." (John Maxwell)[41]

7. **Use caution in counseling.** According to one study, more than 80 percent of cases of moral failure of pastors and leaders begin in the context of counseling. A wise Christian counselor will never counsel a person of the opposite sex alone, especially with the door closed. Whenever possible, do counseling with your spouse or another person present.

Often, persons seeking advice open their hearts to the counselor, sharing things of a personal and intimate nature. This requires much wisdom and discretion on the part of the counselor. As stated before, some persons are vulnerable to the attention, misinterpret it, and fall in love with the counselor, who now not only *has* the answers but *is* the answer. If the counselor is unguarded or vulnerable, both are sitting on a time bomb. A pastor who works with fallen leaders told of a pastor who called him and said, "Bill, I have been counseling a woman from my church for some time, and one day…well, it happened!"[42] The time bomb detonated.

A young woman came to us for help in Mexico City. My wife, Annis, and I listened as she shared how her pastor, in a "counseling session," took her to the second floor of the church (where no one else was present), spoke to her, and then hugged her for almost half an hour. Needless to say, this kind of "pastoral therapy" has no place in ministries of integrity. Both counselors and counselees should be aware of warning signs. According to family counselor

---

[41] John Maxwell, speaking to thousands of men in a Promise Keepers stadium rally in 2002.
[42] Don Crossland, *Refocusing Your Passions* (Nashville, Tennessee: Star Song Publishing Group, 1994), 23.

Dr. Patrick Carnes, more than 50 percent of women with sexual problems manifest sexual tendencies toward counselors during counseling sessions.[43] Wise leaders will take necessary precautions to avoid situations like these.

8. **Learn to detect and reject improper influences.** Here is a good rule of thumb: *When any influence, in any form, in any measure, comes to extinguish or diminish my love for my mate, or to transfer my affection to another person, it is the spirit of fornication, of seduction, of infidelity, that is operating. Whether it is a look, a touch or caress, a word, a feeling, a thought, "vibrations," a fantasy, an image, flirting, or any other gesture, it is to be rejected immediately.*

We must be alert to the spiritual radar God has placed within us, detecting and rejecting intrusive influences. God's Word guarantees that he who plays with fire will be burned. In an oft-quoted text in Proverbs, Solomon asks: "Can a man take fire to his bosom, and his clothes not be burned? Can one walk on hot coals, and his feet not be seared?" (Proverbs 6:27–28).

> *We must be alert to the spiritual radar God has placed within us, detecting and rejecting intrusive influences.*

Sexual sin is very deceitful (see Hebrews 3:13). It promises much but delivers nothing but pain, regret, and hurt. In place of happiness, it dispenses misery. In place of liberty, captivity. Instead of lifting us, it pushes us into quicksand. In place of solutions, it exacerbates our problems. Falling prey to the deceitfulness of temptation puts

---

[43] Patrick Carnes, quoted by Mark Laaser in the course: "Sexual Addiction," of Light University, Forest, Virginia, Study Manual, 11.

us on dangerous curves where our life, our marriage, our family, our testimony, and our ministry can crash and burn.

9. **Reject the practice of a double standard.** "Two sets of rules—one for the people—another for me." It's easy for leaders to fall into this perverted thinking: "I'm the leader. I'm special and privileged. I don't have to obey the rules of conduct like the others. My leadership position gives me certain rights and privileges. I live in the grace of God, in a special relationship to Him, and He overlooks my occasional slipups. I live on a higher level and don't need those rules like others do." One church leader, along with some of his male staff, engaged in sexual relations with women counselees. They told the women, "Don't say anything about this to others. It's all right for us, but they are not on the same spiritual level as we are, and they wouldn't understand." In other words: What is wrong for others is all right for us—a classic double standard. That false concept has led to the moral fall of many. The truth is, God expects more of leaders, not less.

10. **Learn to do battle.** We cannot be passive and win the battle against lust. There are malignant forces that come against us that must be rejected and resisted in the powerful name of Jesus. Passivity—the no-action stance—gives an advantage to the enemy and puts us on the defensive. We must take the offense when dealing with sexual sin. James 4:7b exhorts us: "Resist the devil and he will flee from you." Nehemiah faced merciless opposition when carrying out his assignment of rebuilding the destroyed wall of Jerusalem. Attack after attack was successfully resisted. The secret? In Nehemiah 4:14, this great leader told the people, "Do not be afraid of them. Remember the Lord, great and awesome, and fight for your brethren, your sons, your daughters, your wives, and your houses." So arise, take up

your arms, and fight the good fight of faith. You can win when you fight in the power of the Holy Spirit and in the name of Christ!

In 1938, Prime Minister of England, Winston Churchill, stood before the parliament of his nation. England was under the threat of Hitler's brutal aerial attacks. Members of parliament were passive and reluctant to declare war. But Churchill recognized that war was inevitable if their nation was to remain free. In his speech, he expressed these immortal words: "We must choose between war and dishonor."[44]

> *We must choose between war and dishonor. Winston Churchill*

To do nothing was synonymous with defeat and dishonor. The alternative—declaring war—could bring victory. England accepted the challenge, squelched Hitler's attacks, and helped win World War II. Today, England is a free country. For the believer, Churchill's words ring true today: we must choose between warring with the enemy and winning or suffering the dishonor of defeat. The dictionary defines war as "a struggle between opposing forces… for a particular end." The "end" is total victory and a life of moral purity and sexual integrity. Our destiny in God is victory. Let us not lose the crown promised to those who overcome. He says we are "more than conquerors" through Christ and the power of the Holy Spirit. He is at our side, fighting our battles with us and giving us triumph in every combat. Remember: We too must choose between war and dishonor!

---

[44] Joe Dallas, *The Game Plan* (W Publishing Group, a Division of Thomas Nelson Publishers, 2005), 89.

11. **Cultivate the fear of the Lord in your life.** Conference speaker John Bevere tells of visiting Jim Bakker in a federal prison. Bakker had been a television evangelist but was then imprisoned for financial fraud. He also had had a moral fall. Bevere asked Bakker, "Jim, when did you stop loving Jesus?"

    Bakker replied, "I never stopped loving Jesus. What was lacking was the fear of God in my life."

    What role does the fear of God play in our lives? It helps us shun evil: "In mercy and truth atonement is provided for iniquity; and by the fear of the LORD one departs from evil" (Proverbs 16:6). The fear of God is not being afraid of Him but a profound sense of awe and reverence for the holiness and majesty of His person that leads to obedience. It also indicates a healthy fear of the consequences of disobedience. Exodus 20:20 declares, "And Moses said to the people, 'Do not fear; for God has come to test you, and that His fear may be before you, so that you may not sin.'" In this revealing verse, we see the two kinds of fear: God said, "Do not fear" (that is, do not be afraid or terrified); then "His fear" is the healthy awe of Him that keeps us from veering off the road on a hazardous curve. The fear of the Lord keeps us from wrong choices and actions. Choose the way of obedience and the fear of the Lord. It is the way of the wise. "A wise man fears and departs from evil, but a fool rages and is self-confident" (Proverbs 14:16).

Conclusion: Finishing Well

Close the doors! One day in March 1987, the ferry *The Herald* boarded its passengers and cars for another routine trip across the English Channel. To embark on the crossing, the large door of the bow had to be closed. Was it negligence, forgetfulness, distractions?

DANGEROUS CURVES

For an unknown reason, the door that day remained open. When the captain gave the go signal, the ferry launched its last, ill-fated journey across the channel. Within minutes, the vessel filled with water and sank. That day, 193 persons lost their lives, along with many cars, personal property, and the ferry itself. All this horrendous loss for the apparent "slipup" of failing to close a door!

How many lives, marriages, families, and ministries have become engulfed in the waters of immorality! An open door is an invitation to disaster. The Bible tells us to give no place to the devil (Ephesians 4:27). If there are any doors open in your life, in thought, feelings, or practice, please take the road of wisdom and close them. Temptation is subtle and searches for openings to our mind and heart. In 2 Corinthians 2:11, it counsels us to never let Satan take advantage of us, that "we are not ignorant of his devices." The waters of illicit sex will sink our "vessel" if we do not take the precaution of closing and bolting the door.

The search for love, sexual pleasure, and intimate companionship outside of God's plan will never fill the vacuum in our lives. It will be like the carob pods—the swines' feed—that the prodigal son desired to eat. They are cheap substitutes that can never truly satisfy us. The prodigal son remembered the good food in his father's house and decided to return. The man or woman who is willing to abandon sexual misconduct and turn to Christ will find in Him a faithful *friend* who desires to help.

> *When we give Him control of our life, the hazardous curves no longer threaten us because He is driving.*

He can and will liberate the truly repentant person from the clutches of illicit sex, whatever its form. And then, having rescued us from the dangerous curves of incautious living, He will guide us into pathways of moral purity and sexual integrity. When we give Him control of our life, the hazardous curves no longer threaten because He is driving.

Stay awake! In 1862, French military forces invaded Mexico. During their march on Mexico City, they camped in the central park of the city of Orizaba, in the state of Veracruz. Mexican army troops were stationed on a nearby hill called Cerro del Borrego (Hill of the Sheep). Having planned a siege for the following day, they settled in for a night's rest on the summit of the hill. Believing there was virtually no danger of an attack by the French soldiers, they failed to post lookout guards around their camp and proceeded to enjoy a good night's sleep. During the night, however, the French *did* attack. Lack of vigilance, overconfidence, and carelessness were the fatal errors of the Mexican commander and resulted in as many as two thousand of his troops being annihilated. While they slept, the enemy attacked.

> And…knowing the time, that now *it is* high time to awake out of sleep; for now our salvation *is* nearer than when we *first* believed. (Romans 13:11)

> Therefore let us not sleep, as others do, but let us watch and be sober. (1 Thessalonians 5:6)

More than one battle has been lost due to sleeping guards. More than one ministry, marriage, or opportunity has been lost for lack of vigilance in our moral journey through this life. Dangerous curves have been the undoing of many a traveler who failed to heed and obey the warning signs. As you negotiate those curves in your journey, remember: God is with you. He loves you; He longs to see you reach your destiny—a life of moral purity. You *can* finish well! "Guard your heart with all diligence, for out of it spring the issues that determine the quality and direction of your life." (Proverbs 4:23, paraphrase).

DANGEROUS CURVES

Finish the Race with Honor

In an earlier chapter, I mentioned Samson, who "began" to deliver Israel, but who eventually had a tragic end. King Saul started well but finished a colossal disaster. Like them, thousands of believers and spiritual leaders have begun well and ended in shipwreck. Sexual sin was a time bomb that shattered what could have been a fruitful and honorable ministry.

> *Sexual sin was a time bomb that shattered what could have been a fruitful and honorable ministry.*

A priority of the apostle Paul was to finish his course with honor, dignity, and joy. Note his words from Acts 20:24, "However, I consider my life worth nothing to me; my only aim is to finish the race and complete the task the Lord Jesus has given me" (NIV). In another place, Paul said, "I have fought the good fight, I have finished the race, I have kept the faith" (2 Timothy 4:7). The New Living Translation says it like this: "I have fought the good fight, I have finished the race, and I have remained faithful." What challenging words. May that be the passion of every believer and servant of God!

There is no joy that compares to that of finishing our course well, knowing we have been faithful. Hearing Jesus say, "Well done, faithful servant...enter into the joy of your Lord," will be worth every effort we make to resist temptation and follow the way of moral integrity. Many highway travelers never made it to their destination. A small cross marks the spot where each perished, usually on a dangerous curve. Each cross represents an unnecessary tragedy and provides an invaluable lesson for us: Dangerous curves also exist in the moral sphere, but we don't have to be another casualty. Let us ask God for a clean mind, a pure heart, and a passion for purity and integrity. "He who calls you is faithful, who also will do it" (1 Thessalonians 5:24).

For Reflection

1. Is there an evident passion for God in your life? If not, what hinders you from cultivating intimate communion with Him?
2. Why is it important to separate ourselves from persons, places, or objects that have presented a danger to our moral life in the past?
3. Are you establishing spiritual guardrails in your moral life? What are they? What measures have you taken to protect yourself from a moral fall?

ABOUT THE AUTHOR

Larry Schnedler has served in Christian ministry for sixty years in the United States and Latin America. As a pastor to pastors, his vision is the equipping of pastors and leaders, and his passion is seeing them reach their full potential. He received a master's degree in biblical studies and apostolic ministry and has completed special courses on "Healthy Sexuality" and "Treatment of Sexual Addiction" from Light University. He has taught many seminars on marriage and family issues and has written four books in Spanish. Larry and his wife, Annis, have been married for fifty-seven years and now reside in San Antonio, Texas. They have two sons, Steven and Randy, and three grandsons.

CPSIA information can be obtained
at www.ICGtesting.com
Printed in the USA
BVHW020003110820
586027BV00002B/2